D0501781

CHAMPIONS WAY

CHAMPIONS WAY

Football, Florida, and
the Lost Soul
of College Sports

MIKE McINTIRE

W. W. NORTON & COMPANY

Independent Publishers Since 1923

New York | London

For information about permission to reproduce selections from this book, write to
Permissions, W. W. Norton & Company, Inc., 500 Fifth Avenue, New York, NY 10110

For information about special discounts for bulk purchases, please contact
W. W. Norton Special Sales at specialsales@wwnorton.com or 800-233-4830

Manufacturing by LSC Communications, Harrisonburg
Book design by Chris Welch
Production manager: Anna Oler

ISBN 978-0-393-29261-9

W. W. Norton & Company, Inc.
500 Fifth Avenue, New York, N.Y. 10110
www.wwnorton.com

W. W. Norton & Company Ltd.
15 Carlisle Street, London W1D 3BS

1 2 3 4 5 6 7 8 9 0

To Maggie, without whose love and support this would not have been possible.

And to Walt, the best journalism partner and mentor one could hope for.

CONTENTS

BIG TIME

SOMETHING'S WRONG

PREFACE

The gambler on the phone was threatening to kill me. And break my legs, though not necessarily in that order.

This was the late 1990s, and I had little experience writing about sports. I did know about corruption, however, which was why I had been asked to do a story about a wannabe sports agent accused of showering cash and gifts on promising basketball players at public universities in Connecticut and Massachusetts, including future NBA stars Marcus Camby and Ray Allen. My talent, if you could call it that, was ferreting out white-collar crime. Sweetheart real estate deals for state lawmakers, a briefcase of cash for the mayor, campaign checks from phony donors—that sort of thing. I did enjoy following pro football and baseball, but a college game was mainly for passing the time in front of the television on a rainy Saturday.

So, with no connections in the world of college athletics, I fell back on what I normally did. I searched public records, and eventually wound up in the clerk's office at federal court in Connecticut, examining a petition for Chapter 7 bankruptcy filed by the sports agent. Seems he had borrowed a lot of money to finance his efforts to ingratiate himself with players. Among the

$100,000 in debts he listed were loans from a couple of guys who liked to place bets on college games—raising the possibility that gambling money had made its way into the pockets of student-athletes, a mortal sin under the rules of intercollegiate play.

Now, one of those sports bettors was on the line, insisting that if I put his name in the paper he would drive to the newsroom and shoot me in the head.

"I swear to fucking God," he shouted, "I will blow your fucking brains out!"

What to do?

I decided that transparency was the best defense. When the story was published, I included his threats, figuring that if I later turned up dead, I would have at least been able to leave a big fat trail marker pointing to my likely killer. As it happened, I needn't have worried—I never heard from that guy again. My real enemy was one I hadn't even seen coming: the legion of rabid fans of University of Connecticut basketball who called to curse me out, make crude threats, and hurl insults. They weren't concerned that young athletes had taken money, jewelry, and plane tickets from an unscrupulous hustler with connections to gamblers. Rather, they were upset that I had drawn attention to it and besmirched the reputation of their beloved team. They took it personally.

I didn't know it at the time, but I had just lost my virginity as a sports journalist. I quickly determined that it wasn't something I wanted to repeat any time soon, so for years afterward I stuck to the relative safety of outing crooked politicians, most of whom did not enjoy a fan base sufficiently motivated to harass reporters. Still, the experience had left an impression—and it was not a good one.

Professional sports, to me, had always seemed like the place to expect occasional unsavory headlines. The NFL or NBA player caught with a gun or punching his girlfriend or doing drugs in his Bentley. It was just a given that in a gold-plated fantasyland of bling, balling, and billion-dollar teams, adults would do stupid things once in a while. But college is supposed to be different.

College is where students who are good at a sport, or at least enjoy it, can play in their spare time to round out their education. Sure, the really good athletes can also use it as a springboard to the pros. But at its core, intercollegiate athletics is intended as a healthy adjunct to the pursuit of an academic degree. Where did I get this crazy idea? From the National Collegiate Athletic Association, the governing body of college sports, which for a century has been saying that "graduating from college is as important an achievement as winning on the field."

But that clearly isn't true. And it never has been.

When fans sit down in front of their sixty-inch high-definition Samsungs for a college game on ESPN or one of the proliferating number of cable networks run by the colleges themselves, they're not hoping to find out how the players are doing in their math classes. They want to be entertained. AT&T, Capital One, and Coca-Cola—all NCAA corporate "champions"—pony up millions to associate their brands with that entertainment, and it isn't the graduation rates of the athletes that interests their marketing departments. Nor is that what university presidents and athletic directors dwell on when reclining in the skyboxes of their new luxury stadiums, hobnobbing with well-heeled boosters who help pay their salaries.

In fact, the modern college athletic department is attached to the school in name only. It functions essentially as a subsidiary of corporate funders, unaccountable private booster groups, and professional marketing giants like IMG and Learfield, which are so embedded at some universities that they use campus offices and control everything from stadium advertising to the coach's radio show. The money to be made is so alluring that Wall Street has jumped in, with private equity firms bankrolling companies that cater to college sports. Along the way, this corporate-athletics complex and its supporters in Congress have bullied the Internal Revenue Service and rewritten the tax code to preserve the fiction that it is all a tax-exempt educational pursuit, instead of a nakedly commercial enterprise.

The mind-boggling financial stakes—the NCAA's Division I alone had revenue of $8 billion in 2013—naturally leads to ethical compromises and the cutting of corners. Much of it occurs outside of public view, in the incremental decisions of administrators to trim academic budgets while borrowing millions for new stadiums, raise athletic fees for all students, and shift or cancel classes to accommodate games. At its worst, the negative effects are manifest in academic cheating scandals, lowered admissions standards for star recruits, and the arrests of players for everything from rape to attempted murder—all poison to the carefully tended reputation of a school.

How did we get to this place at our institutions of higher learning, where education, the law, and even basic morality take a back seat to the rapacious, smashmouth needs of the multibillion-dollar business empire known, quaintly, as intercollegiate athletics?

It only makes sense if you accept that big-time college sports exists as an end unto itself. Certainly it has its benefits. It gives local fans something to cheer, students and alumni feel good about their teams, and for a select few schools there are monetary and institutional rewards. But for the most part, it is simply an entertainment platform, broadcast to millions of viewers who have no attachment to the schools involved and directed by well-paid professionals whose primary mission is to grind out wins.

From its earliest days in the nineteenth century, college football, in particular, has reshaped the perception and reality of American higher education perhaps like nothing else. It came thundering out of the storied campuses of Ivy League schools and steadily conquered public universities, initially bringing with it a trail of dead and injured players, complaints about vice and corruption of the game, and growing conflicts with the academic mission of colleges. Only intervention by President Theodore Roosevelt stemmed some of the physical toll on athletes with the creation of new standards for safer play.

However, broader problems in that evolving world of college athletics remained unaddressed. Today, the roots of those problems stretch far and deep, drawing sustenance from warped cultural and business imperatives that were condemned as far back as 1929 in a Carnegie Foundation study as the "darkest blot upon American college sport." That early inquiry found rampant corruption in recruiting, creeping commercialism, and misplaced priorities on the part of college presidents under the spell of big-time athletics. Sixty years later, the Knight Commission on Intercollegiate Athletics found things had only gotten worse, nourished by a river of television revenue that served to amplify the basest instincts of everyone involved. The head of the commission concluded in 1991 that "sanity had to be restored to this bleak scene and values put back into their proper place."

Collegiate sports officials know this, but are too compromised to enact real change. This is made clear in internal NCAA documents, as well as in depositions from a major lawsuit against them by former players, who argued that they were basically functioning as unpaid entertainers while everyone around them profited. In their own words, when they thought no one else was listening, NCAA officials sent emails to each other admitting things like this: "As we callous our collective consciences to the incremental intrusion of commercialism, 'No, you can't do that' begins to be heard less often."

I didn't set out to write about Florida or football. What interested me was the ever-rising cost of higher education. With one kid in college and two more on the way, I wanted to know why it was so damned expensive. Little did I realize that the path of that inquiry would inevitably disappear down the gaping financial gullet of college sports.

I called Richard Miller,* the former president of my alma mater, Hartwick College, a small liberal arts school in the upstate New York burg of Oneonta. I asked him to explain why the cost of attendance—less than $10,000 a year when I was there in the '80s—had now surpassed $50,000. Dick had since become the mayor of Oneonta and was freer to talk candidly about the subject. To my surprise, one of the first things he cited was athletics.

As an example, Miller told me how Hartwick felt compelled to spend millions to upgrade its sports facilities after one of its competitors, Ithaca College, announced plans for a $65 million athletics center. Ithaca then upped the ante, saying it would add new hardwood basketball and volleyball courts to the mix. Hartwick drew the line at that, but Miller could not convince the trustees to save money by downgrading the school's only Division I sports—men's soccer and women's water polo—to the less costly Division III. In particular, boosters, alumni, and local businesses rose up to oppose the reduction in status for men's soccer, whose history of winning had earned struggling Oneonta the self-proclaimed title of Soccer Town USA.

* Miller died in October 2014.

"It got very emotional," Miller recalled. "The numbers didn't add up, but for a lot of people it was about more than that. And then you had the facilities footrace, trying to keep up with your competitor schools. It's really incredible and it doesn't stop."

If it's that bad at a tiny college in the Catskills where sports isn't even a big priority, I thought, what must it be like at huge universities with high-profile athletics programs? The Virginia legislature, as it turned out, tried to answer this question in a series of lengthy reports on spending at the University of Virginia, released in 2013 with great fanfare and then left on a shelf. Interestingly, the reports found that most spending at public universities isn't even on teaching, but rather in the benignly labeled realm of "auxiliary enterprises," which includes athletics, student housing, and dining. Indeed, these categories have been "the largest driver of spending increases at Virginia institutions," the report concluded.

As for athletics specifically, none of the sports programs at Virginia's fifteen public higher-education institutions generated enough revenue to cover all of their expenses, meaning that "most institutions therefore depend heavily on mandatory student athletic fees to subsidize their athletic programs. On average, 12 percent of what Virginia students paid in tuition and fees in 2012–13 was directed toward intercollegiate athletics." Students coughed up $160 million a year in athletic fees on top of tuition—a 50 percent increase in five years.

Then there's the awkward fact that the two highest-paid public employees in the state were the football coaches of the University of Virginia and Virginia Tech, each pulling down more than $2.5 million a year. But there's a caveat. Most of that money comes not from the schools themselves, but from private booster groups, university foundations, and endorsement contracts. I found this curious. How many other situations can you think of where a public employee, presumably answerable to taxpayers, is paid by private individuals and organizations? To whom are they accountable if someone other than the public is buttering their bread?

It was around this time that I happened to overhear my colleague in the investigative unit at the *New York Times*, Walt Bogdanich, talking about something called the Seminole Boosters. Walt, a three-time Pulitzer Prize winner, is one of those old-school reporters who still prefer to call someone or confront them on their doorstep rather than hide behind an email. He also talks loudly on the phone, and with my desk literally next to his in the newsroom, it's hard not to absorb the gist of his conversations.

For months, he had been reporting on Jameis Winston, the star quarterback for Florida State University who had been accused of rape, but never charged. Walt had produced a blockbuster story detailing how university officials and local police had bungled the Winston investigation. Among other things, he reported that the lead detective on the case had worked side jobs for the Seminole Boosters, a private organization that supports Florida State athletics. The Seminole Boosters also helped pay the salaries of the coaches, the athletic director—even the university president.

Walt and I started brainstorming about this peculiar organization. I was shocked to discover that it had more than $200 million in assets, was tax-exempt and functioned largely outside the control of the university, yet was deeply entwined in the management of its athletic department. What was this group all about? Where did its money and influence come from? Florida State declined to answer many questions about its operations. The school was the happy beneficiary of the Seminole Boosters' largesse and didn't care to know much more than that.

Bait set, I couldn't resist trying to find out more. This is the way investigative reporting works. You start off pursuing one thing, and oftentimes end up far from where you began. And yet, not so far. The money that fuels college sports, after all, was a big part of the phenomenon of rising higher-education costs that I had set out to explore. But that raised another, even more complicated question: Why?

What was it about football and, to a lesser extent, basketball that drove otherwise rational university presidents, politicians, and alumni to suspend the laws of finance and critical thinking, throw away millions of dollars, and gamble the reputations of our citadels of higher learning on the precarious self-control of amped-up, reckless young athletes?

Take Dr. Eric Barron. He is an educated man, a scientist, who spent most of his adult life studying oceans and geology, serving on NASA panels and leading the National Center for Atmospheric Research until taking the helm at Florida State in 2010. Before he assumed the presidency of one of the largest public universities in the country, no one would have mistaken the diminutive, intellectual Dr. Barron for a fire-breathing football fan.

Yet there he was on the night of January 6, 2014, on the field after a rousing nail-biter by the undefeated Seminoles in the BCS National Championship Game—the collegiate equivalent of the Super Bowl—looking somewhat silly with red and yellow war paint on his face and a national champions ball cap jammed on his head. Asked by a TV newsman what he thought of his school's thrilling come-from-behind win, Barron did his best to find some loftier lesson.

"We have this expectation that every play will be perfect, and that we'll march down the field and we'll be successful and we'll completely dominate on the score," he said. "But there's something really sweet about being behind and realizing that you're strong enough and you believe and you can march back and take it back."

All in good fun.

Except, not really. College football is deadly serious business, nowhere more so than at Florida State.

Dr. Barron may have genuinely learned to love Seminoles football. But it wasn't as if he had a choice. Much of his $400,000 salary was paid by the Boosters, whose single-minded goal is increasing sports victories at Florida State. The Boosters wield extraordinary influence. Even Dr. Barron's performance goals, set by the university's trustees—some of whom are members of the Boosters—included finding ways to enhance and support "the partnership" between the private Boosters and the public university.

The Boosters helped build the Seminoles' Doak Campbell Stadium, the largest continuous brick structure in the United States, capable of seating more than 82,000. It is the pride of Tallahassee, Florida's capital. A single home game played there can inject as much as $10 million into the local economy. That means more money for everybody, from the cops working security jobs on game days to the local clubs and restaurants. And a winning season means big bucks for the coach, whose contract is filled with bonuses tied to victories, and the university itself, through television revenue and licensing fees. Vested interests abound.

So when Dr. Barron's national champions took to the field that January evening, they didn't get there by themselves. It was a team effort in a much larger sense of the word. The Seminoles had help from police and prosecutors, professors and administrators, business leaders and alumni, defense lawyers and lobbyists. A whole off-field support network, sweeping up messes, propping up grades, paying for perks, and generally making it possible for Florida State University to stay focused on the pot of gold at the end of the college football rainbow.

How else do allegations of rape, attempted murder, academic fraud, domestic abuse, and other scandals—some of them disclosed here for the first time—go unnoticed, uninvestigated, and unpunished?

This is the untold story of what it takes to make a championship team.

CHAMPIONS WAY

CHAMPIONS WAY

The Florida State University preserves, expands, and dissemi-
nates knowledge in the sciences, technology, arts, humanities,
and professions, while embracing a philosophy of learning
strongly rooted in the traditions of the liberal arts. The university
is dedicated to excellence in teaching, research, creative endeav-
ors, and service. The university strives to instill the strength,
skill, and character essential for lifelong learning, personal
responsibility, and sustained achievement within a community
that fosters free inquiry and embraces diversity.

—Mission Statement, Florida State University

The Dedman School of Hospitality in the College of Business
was located in a rather odd place on Florida State University's campus: the south end zone of the Seminoles' football
stadium, on Champions Way.

To say that the mammoth stadium is the centerpiece of the
campus would be an understatement. It is a monumental structure, designed to evoke what one architecture critic called "colloseum, religious and fortress elements," that has academic and
administrative buildings attached to the sides of it, like barna-

cles clinging to a tanker. The dean of students is there. So is the victim advocate's office, where women who have been sexually assaulted seek counseling. Prospective freshmen are sent to Champions Way to begin their campus tour.

Doak Campbell Stadium is the hot, throbbing heart of Florida State University—and, one could argue, Tallahassee itself. To get to "Tally," gateway to Florida's provincial panhandle, you need to take Interstate 10 for hours, skirting the Deep South underbellies of Georgia to the east or Alabama to the west. At the city limits, drivers are greeted by a sign heralding the national champion Florida State Seminoles football team. If Seminole worship were manifested as chromosomal Xs and Os from a football playbook, it would appear in the braided DNA strands of Tally culture. Whole storefronts are painted garnet and gold. Billboards celebrate the team. People drive around with "National Champion" license plates.

Loyal fans find it inspiring, and the university leadership fully embraces football as key to their school's identity. Others view the whole obsession warily. When the capacity crowd of more than 82,000 unites in a thundering war chant and swings its arms in a "tomahawk chop," as fireworks explode overhead and a Seminole chieftain gallops out onto Bobby Bowden Field to plant a flaming spear into the 50-yard line, an outsider could be forgiven for thinking they were lost in a fascist fever dream.

Christina Lynn Suggs unwittingly entered this world when she accepted a job as a teaching assistant at the Dedman School of Hospitality in 2013. As a forty-seven-year-old mother pursuing a PhD in education, she was not the typical student.

Petite, with an easy smile and a friendly way about her, Christie had always tended toward academic pursuits. She had climbed her way up from small-town Alabama, earning a bachelor's degree in psychology from Auburn in the 1980s, later going back to school to obtain two master's degrees. A hard worker, she was never without a job, and often had more than one: tenured professor at a community college, research technician at a U.S. Army lab, substance abuse counselor, president of the board of a nonprofit suicide prevention service. Former colleagues and students were effusive in their praise of Christie, and comments like "excellent work ethic," "moral and honest," and "compassionate" came easily.

Christie's personal life was not always as bright. Married twice and with frequent money problems, she often suffered from poor health and faced difficulties trying to have children. Once, she filed for bankruptcy, listing tens of thousands of dollars in credit card debts, medical bills, and student loans. When she and her second husband split up, she took with her their young son, Hunter. He was the light of Christie's life and all of her decisions would be shaped around him.

When she decided to return to school again, this time to get her doctorate, she chose a course of study—online distance learning—that enabled her to stay home with her son much of the time. She enrolled in 2008 at Florida State, less than two hours from her home in Dothan, Alabama. Florida State had thrown a lot of resources into the burgeoning field of distance learning, where students do most of their work over the Web, often without ever setting foot inside a classroom. Some online courses had as many as a thousand students.

For her doctoral studies, Christie learned how to develop online classes and ensure their integrity—a frequent rap on distance learning is that it's too easy for students to cheat and difficult for instructors to monitor. She coauthored sophisticated academic papers on educational instructional systems, gave presentations, and received good grades.

As she pursued her degree, she juggled multiple online teaching jobs for Florida State and other schools, cobbling together an income of less than $40,000 while also accumulating an ever-larger pile of student loans. In 2012, she lost her house and moved to an apartment in Tallahassee, where she continued home-schooling ten-year-old Hunter and struggled to complete her doctorate. Like many older PhD candidates who have to balance family, work, and school obligations, Christie found herself in over her head at times. She confided to friends that coming up with a dissertation project was harder than she had imagined, yet she expressed determination to see it through.

By the time she arrived at the Dedman hospitality school, she had a tentative schedule laid out with her advisor to develop a dissertation and complete her degree. She soon found that she was well liked at Dedman and praised for her work. Things were looking up.

Besides literally being situated at the football stadium, the hospitality school had a symbiotic relationship with athletics in other ways, given that its areas of study included the sports, entertainment, and food industries. Among its degree offerings was a major in PGA golf management. Some of its professors had backgrounds in sports management and tourism, which in Florida is closely tied to football, baseball, and golf.

One of those professors was Dr. Mark Bonn, a member of the Florida Tourism Hall of Fame who ran the school's distance learning program. Dr. Bonn appreciated the importance of Florida State athletics, having done studies on the economic benefits of Seminoles football games, which pump millions of dollars into the Tallahassee community. He served for twelve years as a trustee of the Tallahassee Quarterback Club, which gives an annual award—named after football legend and Florida State alum Fred Biletnikoff—to an outstanding college football receiver. He helped host an annual joint fundraiser for Dedman and the Seminole Boosters attended by famous football personalities, such as retired coach Bobby Bowden. And he was friendly with football players, many of whom enrolled in his online courses.

Athletes liked those types of courses because they tended to be easy and flexible, allowing them to do the work on their own time to fit their football schedules. Certainly, the hospitality school offered many traditional business classes that teach students how to manage hotels, restaurants, and resorts. But it was the online courses, in such subjects as the history of wine, that "attract a large number of student athletes," according to a meeting agenda for online teaching assistants from 2013, which said the university expected them to keep a close eye out for players with poor grades.

"Like on-ground classes, we're asked to review athletes' progress on a regular basis and report how they're doing to their academic advisors," the agenda memo said.

Teaching assistants, usually graduate students earning money while in school, are the unheralded grunts of higher education, essentially doing a professor's work but getting paid peanuts. The online courses at Dedman each had an "instructor of record"—usually a tenured professor—but it was the assistants (or TAs, as they are called) who stayed in contact with students, graded assignments and quizzes, prepared course materials, and more. There was also a full-time support staff that managed the teaching assistants' schedules and provided technical assistance and guidance. It was often hard to discern what the professors actually did.

As a teaching assistant in the summer of 2013 for one of Dr.

Bonn's online courses, entitled Coffee, Tea & International Culture, Christie followed protocol and compiled a list of students at risk of failing. Four of them were football players. One of them, defensive end Chris Casher, also struggled in another of Dr. Bonn's online courses, International Wine & Culture. He had missed more than a half dozen quizzes and assignments for that class, blaming it on his need to help his mother while she recovered from surgery.

Casher was informed of his precarious status. In response, he sent in a class project he had needed to complete, a simple Power-Point presentation comparing wine from Chile and Belize. Virtually the entire project was lifted verbatim from online sources like Wikipedia and other web sites. Unsure how to handle this flagrant flouting of academic standards, Christie alerted someone on the support staff in the distance learning program, Aiden Sizemore, who sent an email to Dr. Bonn saying Casher had "copied every portion of his project" with no citations or references listed.

Students who hand in plagiarized work can get into serious trouble. The Florida State web site says students must clearly identify the sources of information they use and, if text is borrowed verbatim, enclose it in quotation marks: "Neglect of these indications shall be considered academic fraud." For athletes, there is an added concern—if they are not in good academic standing, they cannot play. That would be devastating for the football team, which in 2013 was gearing up for a much-anticipated fall season with a retooled lineup of promising players.

It had been more than a decade since the Seminoles had won a national championship, and the university had invested millions to bring its football team back into contention, building a new stadium, hiring a new coach, and showering perks on athletes with the addition of student housing and academic tutors. Academics, in fact, was a big concern. Just a few years earlier, Florida State had suffered an embarrassing scandal involving cheating in online classes that led to forfeited wins for the football team, and many players arrived at school unprepared and overwhelmed with a busy training schedule. Already in 2013 the Seminoles had lost one player on Christie's list of at-risk students, senior receiver Willie Haulstead, because he was deemed academically ineligible.

Dr. Bonn gave Casher a second chance. He told him to use paraphrases and references, and explained how to do it: "Paraphrase means to summarize what an author is saying using your own words. If you copy word for word, it must show what is being used word for word with quotations (" ") before the first word and after the last word." Casher was again late getting his revised work back to Dr. Bonn, who nevertheless accepted it.

Casher then asked if he could make up the rest of his missed quizzes and assignments, which would require the school to reopen his online access to them long after it had been closed. The policy was to allow such access only if a student had a documented excuse approved by the university within two weeks of the absence. In fact, the course syllabus made this clear: "It is *unacceptable* to wait until the last week of class to try and request an extension for coursework due at the beginning of the semester." Dr. Bonn told Christie that Casher "has legit excuses" and to grant him access.

Christie soon found that football players—most of them beneficiaries of athletic scholarships—were frequently being allowed to miss deadlines, turn in subpar or plagiarized work, and make up incompletes in ways that other students were not. After linebacker Terrance Smith missed two weeks of assignments for

Coffee & Tea, Dr. Bonn had Christie reopen his online access to them, saying Smith would give him a medical note later. Three players—Nick Waisome and future NFL picks Timmy Jernigan and Tre' Jackson—finished the spring semester with incompletes, and Dr. Bonn allowed them to make up for them with a joint project over the summer. He told Jernigan in a friendly email to "keep in top shape!" and accepted the project, sort of an imaginary travelogue of Japan and Italy, filled with cut-and-pasted text from Wikipedia.

Receivers Jarred Haggins and Kelvin Benjamin, who later went to the NFL, were each allowed by Dr. Bonn to hand in sections of incomplete projects past the deadline. Benjamin's project contained page after page of text copied wholesale from various web sites that he listed at the end. Haggins at least attempted his own writing:

> Brazilian coffee is one of few places that has a carnival and the coffee place a major role just as much as the dancing and the food. Colombians drink instant coffee and they dint really drink their coffee through out the day.

None of it was college-level work. Dr. Bonn instructed Christie to "take off 15 points and accept." Dr. Bonn's willingness to dock points from the two players for lateness was greeted as a rare victory by school staff.

"If he's enforcing some kind of penalty, then awesome," Aiden Sizemore said to Christie.

But for Christie, a doctoral student in education, coddling truant football players made her increasingly uncomfortable. For one thing, some of them were rude and aggressive with her, complaining when she wouldn't allow them to complete assignments past the deadline. She had to admonish one athlete to "check your tone" when addressing her. More than that, though, their ability to avoid the normal consequences of irresponsible behavior was unfair. After all, her life was at least as difficult as theirs, albeit in different ways. Yet she played by the rules, while they seemed to walk between the raindrops, helped along by a system that placed the primacy of football above the integrity of academics.

Tensions within the distance learning program reached the boiling point with James Wilder Jr., a talented running back who was headed to the NFL and had a history of run-ins with police. He had been arrested three times in the previous year, including for allegedly interfering with a deputy who was trying to take Wilder's former girlfriend into custody. He had to sit out much of spring practice with an injury, but Coach Jimbo Fisher was counting on his return as the fall season approached. Fisher told reporters Wilder had matured.

"When you deal with adversity and realize that things can be taken away from you, it makes you grow," he said. "As a person, that's part of growing up."

In the classroom, however, Wilder continued to have problems. He desperately needed a good grade in the Coffee & Tea course, but had missed some assignments. Rather than contact Christie, his teaching assistant, he reached out to Dr. Bonn directly, saying he wasn't being credited for work "that I know was submitted" and asking that other closed quizzes and assignments be reopened so he could complete them.

"Sorry I had to email you and should have went to the TA but I have worked with you in the past and feel comfortable discussing my academic career with you," Wilder wrote to Dr. Bonn. "With me having my daughter in town I was very busy throughout the semester and wanted to make sure I have everything balanced. Please understand where I am coming from as this last year has been tough for me."

At the bottom of Wilder's email were the answers to two discussion questions that he was submitting late. One was about the sustainability of the Chinese tea industry:

> I think that tea in China isn't sustainable at all it's been getting worse and worse and worse every year there one of the largest producers of tea and that means more money to be giving out its a lot that they need to have done its also a lot of land that have to stay on top of.

Dr. Bonn forwarded Wilder's email to Christie, saying "please use his submissions," and asked her to call him on his cell to talk about Wilder's grade. Christie had explained in a series of emails that there was no hope for Wilder to get the grade he wanted. She detailed the grades on all of his assignments before concluding, "At this point, even if we accept this late work that he emailed you, and he gets 100% on the remaining work, he will still only get a 'D' in the course.

"I have carefully reviewed James Wilder's grades and can assure you that the work he missed is because he did not do it or did not turn it in. I understand he wants a B in the course, but it is my opinion that he should have done the work like everyone else in order to get that grade. Of course, I will be happy to do whatever you want with regards to this situation."

Christie then reached out to Aiden Sizemore, telling him about Dr. Bonn's interest in Wilder. Sizemore was blunt in his response.

"Let me know what he asks of you," he told Christie. "But other than the final project, don't set any adaptive releases unless I say ok first—trying to put a stop to his favoritism for athletes once and for all."

Dr. Bonn exchanged several more emails with Christie asking about Wilder, including one in which he signaled Wilder's importance to the football team: "Let him know what he needs to get a C for the remaining work. If he has excuses for missing his work we may accept them, however let him know he needs to show us excuses. And please copy me on your email to him. He is a starting star running back, however we have to watch out for all of these situations and must adhere to our grading policy for non-athletes and for athletes."

Among other things, Dr. Bonn told Christie to allow Wilder to hand in missing sections of a project past the original deadline. As with the other football players' work, the PowerPoint project was mostly a compilation of cut-and-pasted passages from web sites. According to its digital metadata, the file had been created by a tutor in the athletic department for a different class, International Food & Culture, raising the question of how much of the work was even Wilder's. Concerned that she would be bending the rules, Christie contacted Sizemore again.

"I am not offering this opportunity to other students," she said, "but I will do whatever you guys tell me to do. Thoughts?"

Sizemore said he would take it up directly with the head of the Dedman school, Dr. Jane Ohlin.

"This is above both of our pay grades, lol," he said. "I'll let you know as soon as she responds."

As the hours passed, Christie grew worried. She emailed Sizemore that evening.

"Have you heard anything? I don't want Dr. Bonn to get mad at me for not responding to him. I also don't want him mad at me for not doing what he says. I really want to keep my job."

"Go ahead with what Dr. Bonn wants to do," Sizemore replied, "and just let me know if he tries to have anything else opened without documentation."

Christie did as she was told. Then she made a crucial decision. She would share her concerns about favoritism for athletes with the Florida State University inspector general, the office in charge of rooting out fraud and ensuring integrity in campus operations. Christie Suggs would become a whistle-blower.

THERE'S A
HISTORY HERE

NO. 34

Ashley Witherspoon was one of those diehard 'Noles who would yell at the TV screen during a good game. A bright, athletic twenty-four-year-old originally from Texas, Ashley had embraced college life at Florida State, joining a sorority and spending autumn weekends cheering for the Seminoles football team. She liked to wear the team colors and could do the "tomahawk chop" with the best of them.

Five days before Christmas in 1993, Ashley, who had recently graduated with a degree in English, was feeling good about life. She had plans to get a law degree and was busy preparing for the LSAT. Her Christmas presents were wrapped. And to top it off, her beloved Seminoles were on a roll, close to clinching their first national college football championship.

She was in her apartment near campus in Tallahassee that morning when the doorbell rang. Answering it, she was startled to find a man she did not know. He asked if "John" was home. She said he must have the wrong apartment. "So, John's not home?" he replied. Feeling uneasy, Ashley moved to shut the door, but the stranger, six feet tall and weighing more than two hundred pounds, pushed his way in. He was holding a silver handgun.

Ashley made a grab for the phone, but the intruder ripped it out of the wall and hit her in the face. He went about rifling her purse and gathering up stereo equipment before leading Ashley to the bedroom, where he told her to get on the bed. It was while he was unzipping his pants that the gun went off. Ashley felt a burning sensation in her left breast. In shock and disbelief, she looked at her attacker. She noticed he had a gold tomahawk earring.

"Did you just shoot me?" she said.

He had, but that didn't matter to Michael Gibson. He proceeded to rape Ashley multiple times as the pain and bleeding from the gunshot wound intensified. On his way out, Gibson stopped to rip open a stack of Christmas gifts, looking for anything worth taking. Ashley managed to peer out the window and get a glimpse of his yellow hatchback as he drove off. She caught the first letter of the license plate, an *L*.

Ashley recovered, and nine days later she picked the twenty-one-year-old Gibson out of a police lineup. She also identified items detectives had found in Gibson's apartment that her attacker had worn: a big wristwatch with visible gears and springs, combat boots, a black ball cap. It turned out that he was a serial rapist, eventually charged with attacks on Ashley and three other women. He had held a screwdriver to the throat of one of them as he raped her. Another was assaulted in front of her boyfriend.

That wasn't the Michael Gibson that Ernie and Alice Sims thought they had raised.

The Simses were devout Baptists who preached the Gospel in their free time and had been faithful servants of the Lord Christ since their teens. Ernie and Alice had graduated from Florida State University with degrees in education and put them to use working with young people, often from disadvantaged backgrounds.

And they walked the walk at home as well. In addition to raising two sons of their own, Ernie III and Marcus, the Simses took in a boy who desperately needed a loving family: Michael Gibson. A hulking, moon-faced young man with striking brown eyes, Gibson had been in and out of trouble since he was a little kid. But if there was one thing he was good at, it was football, and so he fit right in with the Sims family.

Ernie had been a running back for the Seminoles back in the day, playing for the legendary coach Bobby Bowden. In fact, it was on the team that he became taken with the Word, as it was so often spoken by the God-fearing Bowden, who was known to read Bible passages at the breakfast table each morning. Alice was an excellent athlete in her own right, having been a track star in college.

With his adoptive parents' encouragement and support, Gibson became a top-notch running back at North Florida Christian High School in Tallahassee. He was No. 34, barreling down the field, juking past defenders on his way to the end zone. Ernie and Alice could not have been more proud when Coach Bowden, with ever an eye for talent, recruited Gibson with a coveted athletic scholarship to play for the Florida State Seminoles in 1992. But even then, there were disturbing forewarnings of trouble with Gibson.

The police later told Ashley that while in high school, Gibson and been accused of assaulting a girl, part of a record of criminal and behavioral issues dating to when he was just eleven years old. Did Bowden know any of this before bringing him to Tallahassee? Certainly he was not averse to bending academic standards to get the talent he wanted. Many schools will make allowances for exceptional athletic recruits who can't make the grade academically, offering them tutoring and other services. Bowden showed few qualms about pushing that envelope.

"It's not uncommon for a coach to come over and say, 'You've got to let this one in, he can go to Washington or Ohio State or wherever,' and I'm sure somebody at Ohio State is saying, 'You've got to let him in because he can go to Florida State,'" said T. K. Wetherell, president of Florida State during the final years of the Bowden era. "Well, that's probably true on any given one, but Bobby has got a list of twenty of them that he wants. I say, wait a minute, we can't handle twenty-five, we're talking one or two here."

Sure enough, trouble trailed Gibson like mud on a shoe, and he only lasted one season at Florida State before unexplained problems—what they were has never been made clear—forced him to leave school. Within a year, he had raped, robbed, and brutalized at least three women—until he met his match with Ashley. Tough and resilient, she was determined from the moment she was left for dead in her bedroom that she would stop her attacker from hurting anyone else. Having the presence of mind to note the first letter *L* of the license plate on his car, Ashley helped seal his fate.

When the police later interviewed Gibson about his whereabouts on the morning of December 20, 1993, he claimed he had gone to bed not long after midnight and didn't wake up till noon. But a friend who had slept at Gibson's apartment that night recalled awakening about 7:30 a.m. to find Gibson up and about, having just returned from somewhere. The friend's car keys, normally in his pants pocket, were on a table, and the car was parked outside the front door. It was a yellow 1984 Fiesta hatchback, plate number LKA4402—the same car Ashley had seen.

Gibson had the added misfortune to face William Meggs as his prosecutor. Meggs, whom everyone knew as Willie, had been a fixture in Tallahassee law enforcement since his childhood days, when he hung around the Leon County lockup, where his father was a jailer. He became a cop in the 1960s and served in the U.S. Marine Corps Reserve. Later, he got a law degree from Florida State University—where everybody in Tallahassee government and politics seemed to go to school—and was elected as the top prosecutor for the 2nd Judicial Circuit in 1985.

His craggy face bracketed by big ears, unruly eyebrows, and receding hair, Meggs carried a reputation for being blunt and fearless, with little sympathy for serious offenders. He once charged a police chief's wife with involvement in a murder-for-hire plot and accused a former speaker of Florida's state house of illegally steering millions of tax dollars to an airport project involving a friend. He also showed few qualms about prosecuting athletes, despite Tallahassee's reputation for tolerating mayhem by members of its beloved Florida State football team.

Meggs also knew his community. Tallahassee may be the capital city, but it retains a small-town insularity and connectedness, a sense that you can see a familiar face in the grocery store or on the pages of the newspaper. Having followed youth sports— he once coached a pee-wee football team—Meggs recognized Michael Gibson even before he landed in jail.

"I knew his reputation as a high school student," he recalled. "He was kind of the prima donna. There was sort of a reputation there that wasn't all good. I'd heard he'd gotten angry over the outcome of a game once and started throwing a trash can around or something in the gym."

Ashley found comfort in Meggs's determination to nail Gibson to the wall.

"Willie really was my hero," she said. "I've called him my knight in armor, and that's what he was to me. I couldn't have asked for a better champion."

Meggs was true to his word. Michael Gibson was convicted of attempted murder, multiple counts of sexual assault, armed robbery, and other offenses, and sent to prison with six life sentences. Ashley felt confident she'd seen the last of him.

She hadn't.

"Where it all begins!"

That used to be the mantra in ads for Foot Locker, a popular sports apparel store in Tallahassee in the 1990s. It would also come to hold special meaning for the legacy of Bobby Bowden and Florida State football—and not in a good way.

Bowden, more than any other figure in the history of Florida State athletics, was responsible for building the Seminoles brand into what it is today. It occurred almost by happenstance.

He first joined the Seminoles as an assistant coach in 1962, having come from Alabama, where he had compiled a winning record at a small school called Howard College. At that time, Florida State football was just beginning to find itself. The team had disbanded early in the twentieth century after a reorganization of the state's public colleges, and it didn't resurface again until after World War II, amid another shakeup that created Florida State University out of what had been the Florida State College for Women. With the addition of male students to the school came the resurrection of football in 1947.

After just three years in Tallahassee, Bowden left to coach at West Virginia. During his time away, Florida State athletics went through an upheaval in the late 1960s when the football coach, Bill Peterson, recruited the first two black players in the school's history. The pair were targeted by a campaign of racist harassment, leading one of them, Ernest Cook Jr., to change his mind and sign with a school up north. The other player, Calvin Patterson, toughed it out, but his time in Tallahassee ended tragically in 1972, when he died from a self-inflicted gunshot wound to the stomach, an apparent suicide.

Besides tearing down the color barrier, Coach Peterson won games and put Florida State football on the map. But his successors produced losing records, until Bowden returned in 1976, this time as head coach. By his second season, he had turned the team around, won a bowl game, and infused the program with a newfound sense of optimism and confidence. He would go on to create a football dynasty, taking the school to five national championship games and winning two of them. It wasn't the culmination of a grand plan. It just sort of happened.

In 1994, the Seminoles captured the first of those championships—the one Ashley had looked forward to watching before her life was shattered by Michael Gibson. Bowden was riding high. He had ached for the national title, obsessed over the fact that in his long career he had never won one. Before the game, he quipped to reporters, "Imagine what they'll say even if we do win—'You're sixty-four years old and you haven't even won *two*.'"

But he had barely had a chance to bask in the glow when a scandal exploded onto the cover of *Sports Illustrated*: "Tainted Title: The inside story of how Florida State football players sullied their national championship by taking illicit cash and gifts from agents." The story laid out in devastating detail how a crew of slimy operators had found willing takers on the Florida State team, including what became a notorious episode in which nearly a dozen players were given a $6,000 shopping spree at a Tallahassee Foot Locker ("Where it all begins!"). And, as with the recruitment of Gibson, there were questions about how much Seminoles coaches knew or should have known.

Amid the fallout, Florida State's longtime nemesis Steve Spurrier, head coach of the University of Florida Gators, self-servingly gave voice to a growing feeling that corners were being cut in Bowden's shop. Joking that FSU stood for Free Shoes University, Spurrier recounted a comment made by the mother of an athlete he was trying to recruit: "She told me, 'The cars in your parking lot don't look as good as the ones at FSU.' I told her she was right and that ours are never going to look that good. I don't know how [FSU players] get new cars, but they have a way of getting them."

He added: "There is a perception out there about them. And it's a perception around the country, not just me. Good things seem to happen to their players with regards to material things once they get there."

There were other, more serious problems. Within months of kicking the winning field goal for Florida State in the 1994 national championship game, Scott Bentley was charged with illegally taping a sexual encounter with another student and then playing it for teammates. Bentley argued that he had made the tape as insurance, in case the girl later tried to claim the sex wasn't consensual. Meanwhile, another Florida State player, Kamari Charlton, was charged with sexual assault after a former girlfriend said he grabbed her by the throat and raped her.

Bowden suspended both players, although they were allowed to remain on scholarship with full room and board pending the outcome of their cases. The coach trumpeted it as a victory for women.

"This," he said, "should serve as a clear message to our football players that this behavior and mistreatment of women will not be tolerated."

It wasn't long, however, before Bowden reinstated both of them. Bentley, who had to do forty days of community service, never missed a game because his summer suspension was lifted before the fall season started. And Charlton was back on the team the following season after he was acquitted at trial. He would be arrested again a few years later, this time for battery, and sentenced to community service.

There is no doubt that the Bowden era saw Florida State's football fortunes skyrocket. The team under his leadership peaked in the 1990s, winning at least ten games a season and ending the decade's final year with a perfect record. Along the way, the athletic department accrued power and wealth that would have been unimaginable to his predecessors.

But the drive to win was accompanied by a corrosion of the team's—and the school's—reputation. It only got worse as the decade wore on. Between 1997 and 1999, at least eleven football players were arrested for drugs, theft, and other offenses. People started referring to the team as the "Criminoles."

It was an odd paradox. Head coach for thirty-three years, Bowden is revered in college sports as not only a master of the game, but also a decent man, not given to the bombast and intemperance of some of his hot-headed peers. By all outward appearances, the gentlemanly Bowden, for whom "dadgummit" was the limit of his profanity, did not fit the archetype of the raging, red-faced, win-at-all-costs coach.

And yet, he kept taking risks—and was up front about it. Questioned by a reporter in 1999 about the embarrassing scandal involving sports agents plying his team members with cash, Bowden said, "That's one of the prices of being number one or number two.

"Some other schools say, 'It don't happen to us.' You know what their problem is? They don't have any good football players."

What drove Bowden? National title in hand and four decades in coaching under his belt, he might have been expected to ease up and start thinking about retirement as the twenty-first century approached.

But Bobby Bowden was being pursued by another demon, this one in the form of another old coach, with whom he was locked in an all-consuming race to record the most career wins in college football. His name was Joe Paterno—and he had some demons of his own.

JUST ONE MORE

Z.K. was excited to be visiting the mighty Penn State football locker room. An eleven-year-old who lived with his mother and sisters and attended a local program for underprivileged youths, Z.K. was a big fan of the Nittany Lions.

His tour guide that day in May 1998 was none other than Jerry Sandusky, the youth program's founder and a well-known face at Penn State, where he roamed the sidelines as assistant to the great Joe Paterno, the winningest active coach in Division I college football. Sandusky took the boy around the empty athletic facilities, impressing Z.K. by letting him try on players' helmets and use the training equipment. After kicking a ball around and showing the boy some wrestling moves, Sandusky announced it was time to hit the showers.

Feeling a little uncomfortable, Z.K. got undressed in one of the locker rooms and went, with a towel wrapped around him, to the showers. Sandusky was already there. The coach stood under one shower and had turned on another one beside him. Z.K. went to a different shower, but Sandusky asked him to use the one beside him, saying he'd already warmed it up.

Sandusky told jokes and tickled Z.K. under his arms and on

his stomach. He grabbed the boy around the waist and lifted him up, pretending to be a monster, growling and saying playfully, "I'm going to squeeze your guts out!" His chest hairs were in Z.K.'s face.

Setting him down, Sandusky said they needed to get soaped up, and he offered to rub soap around Z.K.'s back where he couldn't reach. Then he lifted him up again to rinse the lather out of the boy's hair. Later, Z.K. recalled that his chest was against the coach's chest.

"And that's the last thing I remember about being in the shower. It's just kind of black."

Z.K.'s mother reported Sandusky's molestation of her son to the campus police. The cops investigated and had little doubt that the assault had occurred—Sandusky admitted the basic facts and even said he had done similar things with other children in the past. He asked Z.K.'s mother for forgiveness and told her, "I wish I were dead." Coach Paterno and the university president were made aware of the incident.

But Penn State officials were not in the habit of doing anything to tarnish the Nittany Lions brand and its iconic public face, "JoePa," as Paterno was affectionately known. So nothing came of it. Paterno kept Sandusky on the team, and even gave consideration to his proposal to start a youth football camp through Penn State. The following year, Sandusky sexually assaulted another boy while at the Alamo Bowl in Texas, and the year after that, campus janitors caught him violating yet another child in the same showers where he molested Z.K. The janitors kept it to themselves, one of them explaining later that "football runs this university" and that he feared that "Paterno has so much power, if he wanted to get rid of someone, I would have been gone."

Paterno did have outsized influence at Penn State, and in the world of college sports in general. At Penn State since 1950, he had more wins than any other football coach alive and couldn't conceive of quitting, especially amid sports chatter that his slightly younger rival, Florida State's Bobby Bowden, would most likely surpass him in the wins column before their geriatric contest was over.

The rivalry between the two old coaches had taken on historic proportions. Bowl games were arranged around it, with big money at stake. When Florida State and Penn State squared off in the Blockbuster Bowl in 1990, each team was looking at a $1.6 million payout just for appearing. The television announcer highlighted the coaching rivalry, noting it was the twenty-fifth season as head coach for each of them—a silver anniversary: "It's Paterno and Bowden, on the same silver field—and it promises to be a Blockbuster smash!" Florida State won, 24–17, nudging Bowden closer to Paterno in the wins column, 205 to 229.

By the start of the twenty-first century, Paterno seemed to be on the wane—the year 2000 handed him his first losing season in twelve years and no bowl appearance. It looked like Bowden would soon surpass him in career wins. Plans were in the works to erect a bronze statue of Paterno on campus, a sure sign that the university, while appreciative, believed the sun was setting on the JoePa era.

On a Saturday morning in February 2001, Paterno received a visitor to his home. It was during the all-important recruiting period when college coaches are trying to lure high school prospects. Just a few days before, a Florida newspaper had run a story crowing about how Bowden had beaten Paterno so far in signing the best players. Now, a graduate assistant and team aide was at Paterno's door, with the disturbing news that he had seen Sandusky assaulting a boy in the shower. Again.

Paterno, like Bowden, was a religious man. More than once, he had had his wife reassure the mothers of athletes he was recruiting that the Paternos were Catholic and would guarantee their sons went to church. An Ivy League–educated classicist with a reputation for integrity, he also was known for not tolerating foolish behavior on his team. So it would not have been surprising for him to go to the police, or to confront Sandusky and demand the name of the child.

But he didn't. Instead, he waited a day and then told only his immediate superiors at the university. Then, just as in 1998, Paterno and other Penn State officials failed to do the right thing. No one tried to learn the identity of the victim, inform child protection authorities, or ban Sandusky from the athletic facilities. It would take another ten years, and two more known victims, before Sandusky was finally stopped.

In the never-ending race against Paterno and other elite coaches to recruit the best high school football prospects, Bobby Bowden, like his peers, could supplicate himself when necessary to get what he wanted. And as the start of the 2003 season approached, he desperately wanted Ernie Sims III—the brother of Michael Gibson, who was sitting in jail with a life sentence for the attacks on Ashley Witherspoon and other women.

It had been ten years since Gibson's arrest, and now his attorney was making use of a recent change in state law that invalidated one of the charges he was convicted of—attempted felony murder—to appeal his life sentence, arguing he should be resentenced to forty years instead. Papers had been filed with the court and letters of support from family and friends were being gathered on his behalf, in anticipation of a hearing that October.

Ashley was shocked. The thought of her tormentor getting out of prison left her terrified. If that weren't bad enough, she would have to relive the trauma in court, again. She had worked so hard to move on with her life. After the attack, she had left Florida for law school in another state, where she met and eventually married a fellow law student. The two of them opened a family law practice and were busy raising two children.

The Sims family had tried to move on, too. In the wake of Gibson's crimes and punishment, Ernie and Alice found solace in their religious faith. Ernie was ordained at the Fellowship Independent Baptist Church in 1995, began serving in a juvenile detention center ministry and started the W.A.Y. Ministries of Tallahassee, where Alice also assisted. And they redoubled their attention to their three remaining children at home.

Ernie III and Marcus had followed Michael and their father into football. Ernie III, in particular, showed tremendous promise. He was not physically huge for a linebacker—six feet, 225 pounds—but he was strong as an ox and able to inflict bruising tackles, making him the nation's top recruiting prospect while at North Florida Christian High School, where he wore No. 34—the same jersey Gibson had worn. That was not a coincidence.

In spite of everything, Ernie III idolized his older brother and wanted to honor him by wearing his old number. His attachment to Michael was so great that when college coaches started coming around in early 2003 to try to recruit him, he let it be known that he had to have No. 34. His father attempted to explain it to a reporter at the time.

"We tried to help Mike, but it just didn't work," the elder Ernie said, adding, "But Mike is very special to Ernie, and that's what this is all about."

Ernie and his son used the family computer to put together a spreadsheet to itemize and weigh different attributes of the university football programs hoping to nab him, including playing time on the field, religion, and academics. One of the schools in the running was Florida State, where Bowden still reigned.

By then, the Seminoles were seen as in decline, coming off two mediocre seasons in a row, losing the Sugar Bowl to Georgia, and beset by off-field arrests and suspensions of players. But the seventy-three-year-old Bowden wasn't ready to throw in the towel, not while he was within striking distance of Paterno, who was seventy-six, in their ongoing struggle for most career wins: Paterno had 336, Bowden 332.

Besides his competitive drive, Bowden had a financial incentive. His contract, which guaranteed him more than $1 million a year, offered additional bonuses for victories. Florida State would pay him $100,000 for reaching a championship game, lesser amounts for other bowls and $250,000 if he made it to his thirtieth season—he'd already earned an extra $50,000 for breaking Alabama coach Paul "Bear" Bryant's record of 323 wins.

A towering figure in the sport—and the highest-paid public employee in the state of Florida—Bowden wanted to go out on top. So he returned to the deep football talent pool of the Sims family for a third time. But there was a problem: jersey No. 34 had been retired by Florida State in honor of the great Ron Sellers, the last Seminole to wear it in the late 1960s. Bowden had to tread carefully, lest he run afoul of National Collegiate Athletic Association rules prohibiting coaches from promising anything of value—even a favorite jersey number—to lure high school recruits. He quietly put a call in to Sellers and asked if the retired NFL pro wouldn't mind if he offered Sims the number. Sellers said no problem.

So when Bowden made his pilgrimage to the Sims household, he brought along a No. 34 jersey; the family was so moved they took a photo to capture the moment. Not long after, Ernie Sims

III announced he would be going to Florida State. Happy as the Sims family was in February 2003, they still faced the uphill battle of trying to get Michael Gibson's sentence reduced when he came up for his court hearing later that year. And returning for another round as crusading avenger was Ashley Witherspoon's knight in armor, Willie Meggs, who was still the chief prosecutor and just as determined to see Gibson remain behind bars for life. Meggs didn't mince words when the day arrived for a judge to hear Gibson's appeal.

"What we have here," Meggs told the judge, as a subdued Gibson sat a few feet away, "is a serial rapist who has raped, we know of, four women. Brutalized them with firearms, physical force, deadly weapons.

"I want to make sure he never gets out."

Ashley, supported by her husband in the courtroom, summoned the courage to take the stand. She recalled the horror of getting shot and being raped, the viciousness of the attack. Even after Gibson shot her, she said, "He continued to taunt me and grind the gun into my skull" as he sexually assaulted her.

"There's not a day that goes by that I don't think about it. The thought of him getting out of prison terrifies me."

When it was his turn, Gibson rose and apologized to his victims: "I hope that one day you can find it in your hearts to forgive me." And he addressed Ashley directly, saying he was "truly sorry and I know I hurt you in unimaginable ways."

A few others also spoke up for Gibson, including his adoptive parents. Alice Sims asked the judge for mercy, saying she believed Gibson "had repented of his sins."

Finally, the judge considered the handful of letters that had been collected on Gibson's behalf. One of them was written on Florida State University Football stationery. It attested to Gibson's character during his short tenure with the Seminoles, saying he had been "no problem," expressed hope that Gibson had learned his lesson in prison, and concluded with a stirring appeal to the judge: "May God direct you in your decision." The letter was signed "Coach Bowden."

Ashley, who had remained a faithful Seminoles fan, was crushed when she learned of the letter. Given a choice between two Florida State alumni—one of them a mother of two and diligent student who overcame an atrocity to continue her education and become a lawyer, the other a vicious criminal with football skills who bombed out of school—the coach had thrown his support to the thug with a sought-after sibling named Ernie Sims III. Bowden never contacted Ashley, even after friends of hers complained to the university about his letter.

"To have to come back ten years later and have Coach Bowden write a letter of support for him—I just couldn't believe it," Ashley said. "The signature really got to me: 'Coach Bowden.' Why did he do that?"

As for Gibson, the judge rejected his appeal and the Sims family left court that day in October 2003 without much hope. But Bowden soon got what he wanted. Two weeks later, a Seminoles victory over Wake Forest finally pushed him past Joe Paterno as winningest coach—and freshman linebacker Ernie Sims III helped make it happen, with ten tackles, earning him the conference title of "rookie of the week."

Tallahassee was so proud that the state legislature passed a bill renaming the university's football gridiron Bobby Bowden Field.

APOLLO 13

The student athlete said, "I can't read."

Looking over his paperwork when he entered the athletic department's academic support program at Florida State University, Dr. Brenda Monk went to her supervisor and asked, "What in the world are we going to do with" him?

Dr. Monk was the assistant director of the program, which was set up to ensure athletes remain eligible to play by helping them with their schoolwork. It is a challenge, because many of them have little interest in or aptitude for hitting the books. Some come from difficult backgrounds, where academics was never a priority and sports was seen as the ticket out. They arrive at college, not through the normal competitive process that emphasizes test scores, class rankings, essays, and the like, but a special route available to promising athletes. Still, NCAA rules require a base level of academic achievement. Enter Dr. Monk.

A former school principal and special-ed teacher from Mississippi with a doctorate in education administration, she joined the Florida State athletic department in 2001 as a "learning specialist," a newly created position. She got a stellar evaluation her first year and was praised by program director Mark Meleney for her work that "greatly enhances our student-athlete retention rates." That was an important goal.

In the intensely competitive hunt for talented athletes, colleges have been lowering the academic bar, hoping to compensate with support services that could keep the recruits from floundering once they get there. Florida State invested heavily in this approach. Within three years of Dr. Monk's hiring, the $1.5-million-a-year academic support program moved to new offices inside the Moore Athletic Center, built with money from a major Seminoles booster and Tallahassee businessman, DeVoe Moore. From 7 a.m. to 9 p.m. every day, the program's thirty-two-station computer lab and eight study rooms hosted about five hundred tutorial sessions for student athletes, mostly football and basketball players.

Dr. Monk estimated that during a six-year period, she assisted 1,200 athletes. About sixty-five of them were considered learning-disabled—including three-quarters of the basketball team and a third of the football team—qualifying them for special assistance. Most were intelligent, some exceptionally so. Dr. Monk recalled one player with a 145 IQ who nevertheless could read only at grade-school level and needed remedial training. Others were in more desperate straits. The athlete who told Dr. Monk he couldn't read was seeking help with an online music appreciation course that many student athletes took because it was easy; among other things, the professor allowed open-book tests.

Still, this particular player could not even read exam questions, so he needed someone to read them to him. Sometimes, as in this case, the severity of a student athlete's problems was so bad Dr. Monk would ask advice from athletic officials on how to offer help without violating NCAA regulations.

"I did seek counsel from the compliance department," she said. "'How can I work with this student? They have a writing disability, they write at the second-grade level. How am I going to be able to accommodate them? What can I do?' "

Reading stories aloud to athletes who could not read on their own was one thing she did.

"If they were unable to read the short story because it was written, say, on the eighth- or ninth-grade level, and maybe they only read on the second-grade level because of the severity of their learning disability, we would read the story."

Helping write up their assignments on the computer was another.

"Sometimes," Dr. Monk said, "they would hand me a draft where their handwriting was so poor and their English was so poor, that for me to be able to talk with the student I had to get it in a format that I could read."

It was tiring and stressful work. And one day in 2007, she cut a corner that would come back to haunt Florida State. Al Thornton, a star Seminoles basketball player who was close to being drafted by the Los Angeles Clippers, had been to the academic support office and written down the answers to a quiz for an online psychology course. He left without properly entering them into the computer. Later, Dr. Monk noticed the oversight, but rather than take care of it herself or track down Thornton, she asked another student athlete in the office to type in the answers for him. The athlete complied, but was not happy about carrying water for the careless big shot, so he complained to an athletic department official.

That triggered an internal investigation that ultimately revealed that sixty-one athletes in ten sports, including twenty-five football players, had received inappropriate help from tutors and advisors in the academic support program. Dr. Monk was accused of helping write papers and providing answers to tests—something she denied—and resigned from Florida State. Two other employees

also left. The scandal, which dragged on for years, was humil-
iating for the university and marked its seventh serious NCAA
infraction since the 1960s. The school faced the prospect of suspended players and, worst of all, forfeited wins for the football
team—potentially undermining Bobby Bowden's septuagenarian
struggle with Joe Paterno for the crown of winningest coach.

At an NCAA hearing, Florida State's president, T. K. Wetherell,
cast the stakes in absurdly grandiose terms, offering insight into
the outsize importance the university placed on athletics.

"I kind of reflect back to *Apollo 13*," he told the NCAA officials,
"and remember that they started off to the moon, and in the
final analysis never made that, but it may well have been NASA's
most probable or best performance of all. I think Florida State
will come out of this a better institution, as embarrassed as we
might be."

Comparisons to space missions notwithstanding, Florida State's
academic cheating scandal was a big deal, if for no other reason
than it peeled back the lid on the elaborate infrastructure colleges created to support athletes in ways not available to other
students. This bifurcated system provides millions of dollars,
staffing, and resources that allow athletes not otherwise eligible
or prepared for college to be recruited by coaches desperate to
get an edge on the competition.

The FedEx Student Athlete Academic Support Center at the
University of Mississippi is a case in point. A $5 million project,
paid for in part with corporate donations, it has "offices, conference rooms, 20 large and small group tutoring rooms, a large
study area, a multi-media classroom, computer lab and 150-seat
high-tech auditorium." A glowing article about it, cranked out by

the university's public relations office, highlighted a white female member of the rifle team, a biology major named Abbey with a 3.74 GPA and plans to attend medical school, saying how she benefited from the "quiet study areas, tutoring services and academic counseling."

A more meaningful anecdote was relegated to the bottom of the story: a black running back named Jeff (no GPA mentioned), majoring in "general studies." The academic support he got at the FedEx Center "has kept Jeff just as excited about his future as he is about the football season," it said. Black male athletes— who comprise 78 percent of the football and basketball teams but only 5 percent of the undergraduate student body at Ole Miss—graduate less than half of the time. As for Jeff, raised by his single father in Miami who got him started in football as a young boy, he eventually got his degree but went undrafted. He was picked up as a free agent by the Cincinnati Bengals in 2014, with the prospect of an NFL minimum rookie salary of about $400,000. However, a month later he was cut from the team, his only guaranteed money the $2,000 signing bonus they gave him. No other NFL team picked him up; recently he was playing in an indoor football league in Nebraska.

At Ohio State University, the athletic department in 2012 started giving out iPads to players and devoting resources to helping them with time management and study skills. Those perks didn't seem to register with Ohio State's third-string quarterback, Cardale Jones, who took to Twitter that year to complain: "Why should we have to go to class if we came here to play FOOTBALL, we ain't come to play SCHOOL classes are POINTLESS." For his outburst of candor, Jones was suspended for a game—but all's been forgiven since he led the Buckeyes to a national championship in 2015.

The NCAA also provides support to athletes through its

Academic Enhancement Fund, which disburses about $26 million a year to Division I universities to help pay for athletic department amenities such as tutoring, laptops, and "salaries and benefits and capital improvements that enhance the academic services." The academic money is actually a drop in the bucket compared to what the NCAA distributes to schools—about $500 million in Division I alone—but nevertheless reflects concerns about the appallingly low graduation rates for some athletes in big-time college sports programs.

Anyone searching for a concrete measurement of academic success among college athletes soon finds themselves in a wilderness of contradictory data and formulas, some of which seem designed to support one conclusion or another. The federal government's official four-year graduation rate for college athletes in 2013 was 65 percent, roughly the same as the overall student population. But drill down into data for individual schools and the picture clouds very quickly.

At Indiana University, the graduation rate for men's basketball players was 8 percent. At Iowa State it was 13 percent. Some of this no doubt reflects the notorious "one-and-done" aspect of college men's basketball, where the best players are recruited with no intention of having them remain in school more than a year before they jump to the pros, their college experience serving as a quick revolving door into the NBA. For football players the numbers are also disturbing, especially for black athletes. A University of Pennsylvania study of graduation rates for black players among teams participating in the 2014 Bowl Championship Series found that Florida State had the worst record, with little more than a third graduating within six years, even though black players made up almost 70 percent of the team.

Even if they do get an education, athletes are not guaranteed it will necessarily be worth much, as Michael McAdoo discovered when he chose to go to the University of North Carolina, known for its high academic standards. Based on his high school record of good grades and student leadership, he should have thrived there.

At Antioch High School in Nashville, McAdoo had been the big man on campus in more ways than one. Standing six feet, seven inches and weighing 220 pounds, he was student council president his senior year, and his grade point average when he graduated in 2008 was a solid B. But it was his athletic skills as an all-star defensive end that got him noticed. An ESPN scouting report called him a "tall lean kid with the build of a praying mantis" and a "very interesting prospect" for college football coaches looking to recruit him. In an interview with the local newspaper, McAdoo was asked about the schools he was considering. "My top five," he said, "are Vanderbilt, North Carolina, South Carolina, Ole Miss, and the University of Tennessee."

Vanderbilt and Tennessee would have been closer to home, where McAdoo was raised in a low-income household by his mother and grandparents. But the University of North Carolina athletic department aggressively pursued him, calling on his family several times in the years before he graduated and culminating in a visit by head football coach Butch Davis and his staff. They stressed the academic advantages of going to North Carolina. Then the visiting North Carolina officials asked if they all might say a prayer together. McAdoo, his mother, grandmother, and grandfather stood and held hands with the coach and his crew in the living room and prayed.

"I can't guarantee that Michael will play in the NFL," Davis told McAdoo's family, "but one thing I can guarantee is that he will get a good education at the University of North Carolina."

McAdoo set off on his five-hundred-mile journey with an athletic scholarship to one of the most prestigious public universities in the country. He looked forward to the possibility of an NFL career, but also the prospect of at least a college degree in criminal justice, his preferred choice for a major. However, no sooner had he arrived than he discovered that the intercollegiate athletic machine had other plans for him.

To accommodate what would be a rigorous schedule of games, practice, and training, McAdoo was steered toward three degree choices: Afro-American studies, communications, or exercise and sports science. The football program had relationships with professors in those departments, he was told, and they understood the needs of athletes. McAdoo didn't know it then, but he had entered a system that would soon be revealed to have institutionalized academic fraud in order to keep athletes eligible to play.

Beginning in 2010, a series of investigations revealed that for eighteen years, the university had allowed two hundred no-show "paper classes" in the African and Afro-American Studies department, which rarely if ever met and involved more than three thousand students. Athletes were funneled into the program, where they breezed through with high marks that bumped up their grade point averages. The university awarded $29 million in athletic scholarships to 584 athletes in the phony courses just from 1998 to 2011. The epic scandal only came to light after a participant, a learning specialist named Mary Willingham, blew the whistle and became a source for the local newspaper. For her efforts, she was publicly smeared by university officials and sports fans, but ultimately proven right by an outside investigator hired by the university, who concluded that school staff "saw the paper classes and the artificially high grades they yielded as key to helping some student-athletes remain eligible."

North Carolina was far from alone—research for this book turned up at least forty academic scandals involving college sports programs since the 1980s. Ironically, it was the University of North Carolina that sounded an early alarm back in 1989, when an ad hoc committee on athletics warned that the effort to recruit athletes "and keep them eligible results frequently in a corruption of the academic process." The ideal of amateur college athletics, it said, had become "overwhelmed by an abundance of money and an intensity of competition and publicity that drive intercollegiate sports toward professionalism."

For its sins, the hard-won reputation of the University of North Carolina took a hit. In the annual Times Higher Education World University Rankings, arguably the most influential barometer of perceived academic standing, North Carolina slipped from forty-first place in 2011 to between sixty-first and seventieth by 2015 (below the top fifty, schools are listed in groups of ten). Not measured in those numbers is the corrosive real-life impact on students like Michael McAdoo.

McAdoo never graduated from North Carolina. In 2010, he was put on academic probation for receiving impermissible help from a tutor for a research paper on Swahili, large portions of which were also apparently lifted from other publications. He was picked up in the NFL supplemental draft by the Baltimore Ravens, but was let go after less than two years and has since struggled to maintain a professional career.

Dr. Kadence Otto has had firsthand experience with the academic challenges black male athletes faced. Now the director of the undergraduate sports management program at Western Carolina University, Dr. Otto taught at Florida State during the Bobby Bowden era while pursuing her doctorate.

Here, in her own words, is what she experienced:

I was sort of starstruck being at Florida State, and then it was like, "Oh my god, what is going on here?" I had a football player in my class who could not read and write. I thought this was unbelievable. There was an academic support tutor who would call every week to check up on the player. I would say, "He's not doing well. He can't read and write." And they said, "Well, we'll see what we can do." That stopped when the player got a career-ending injury. At that point, he's worth nothing to the team, and I never once heard back from the academic support advisor. He never showed up to class again, either.

One of my jobs was to be the class checker. Talk about hand-holding. Basically, my job was to go and make sure they attended class. I had all their schedules, and I literally had a bag of candy. I look in on the class, and make a checkmark if they were there, and give them a lollipop or something. The hand-holding is ridiculous. That's a really low-level developmental motivation. I thought this is really not healthy for these athletes.

The athletes are being exploited, athletically and also academically. The chancellor makes decisions to admit certain people for certain talents, knowingly breaching their standards and putting these kids into a situation that is really untenable. It's hard to take a kid who can't read or write and put him into college-level classes and think he's going to succeed. He can't, and that leads to the next problem, which is they leave the university with a degree and they can't get a job.

Nobody really wants to hear about it. Nobody likes to address the reality that this is what we're doing to these young men, who disproportionately tend to be black. It's not just Florida State. It's widespread. These are institutions that claim to adhere to these lofty values of truth and justice and so on, and yet they are the ones that are engaging in this.

Dr. Otto is far from alone. Tutors and learning specialists saddled with underperforming athletes cannot expect much help from college athletic departments. The departments are concerned with keeping athletes academically eligible to play, but that's about it. The lack of commitment to quality education is evident in the financial incentives to be found in the contracts of coaches and athletic directors, which are heavily stacked in favor of winning games and titles, rather than academic achievement.

At Florida State, the football coach's contract included extra bonuses totaling more than $1 million for such achievements as leading the team to a national championship game ($200,000), winning the championship ($200,000), and being named national coach of the year ($75,000). And then there's this reward if more than 65 percent of the eligible players manage to graduate: $25,000.

One study found that the millions being spent on athletic department academic support centers, while "potentially improving" graduation rates, were also segregating athletes from the broader college experience that other students found beneficial. When athletes did manage to spend time with faculty advisors outside of the athletics sphere, they found the advisors more interested in helping them learn, the study said, adding that athletes "indicated time spent in the athletic academic center negatively affected their ability to connect with faculty, participate in campus organization and community service, and studying."

Adam Weinstein was teaching writing courses at Florida State when he decided to go public with tales of a football program run amok and, in the process, letting down young athletes who had little hope of succeeding after college. Weinstein penned an article for *Deadspin*, in which he memorably described how he and his fellow professors enjoyed Seminoles football, but had grown concerned about the skewed priorities it was inducing.

"We're increasingly flummoxed by the football culture surrounding Tallahassee, one that's grown malignant with the wins and the scrutiny, like a traditional Islamic country turned radical and defensive, its craziest pilgrims whirling around Doak Campbell Stadium, the black cube at the center of their Mecca," Weinstein wrote. "It's a culture that tells these adolescents that their highest calling is to sacrifice their bodies in the grassy shrine, that all else is distraction."

He revealed, among other things, the story of "Lacy," an instructor who complained internally about some problem football players, "including a star receiver, who were turning work in late, cutting corners, submitting seemingly plagiarized work, and pulling childish stunts in her classroom like flipping the lights on and off." Soon after, two of the players confronted Lacy in her office.

"They're both just towering over me and arguing with me. They were puffing their chests and pacing quickly, leaning in on me," Lacy said. "It just felt very, very aggressive. I was very uncomfortable."

Lacy decided not to pursue her complaint much further.

"I was very reticent to fail a football player, because I didn't want to be harassed," she said. "I shouldn't have, but I probably graded them much more easily than the other students."

SECOND CHANCES

Bobby Bowden was a pen pal to more people in trouble with the law than just Michael Gibson.

Over the years, he had lent the stature of his office to other criminally charged football players, including defensive lineman Julian Pittman, who had pleaded no contest to breaking into a female student's apartment through a window and stealing her credit card. Bowden wrote a letter of support to the judge for Pittman's sentencing, which amounted to five years' probation—a lenient punishment that the prosecutor later blamed on Pittman's football connections.

Bowden also took up his pen on behalf of a former Florida State football star, Francis "Monk" Bonasorte, when the latter was being sentenced on federal charges of cocaine distribution. Bonasorte had joined the team under Bowden as a walk-on and unexpectedly became a stellar pass interceptor, making FSU's Hall of Fame, though his collegiate stardom did not translate into a pro career. Instead, he ended up working at a car dealership, where he got caught up in a drug ring and sentenced to prison for six months.

Bowden's support extended to college sports figures beyond

Florida State. He wrote to the football coach of the University of Central Florida, Gene McDowell, who pleaded guilty to lying to federal agents about having tipped off his players that they were being investigated for cell phone fraud. An angry federal judge read aloud in court from Bowden's letter: "Gene," he wrote, "you didn't do any more than a lot of us coaches would have done under the same circumstances." The judge said she hoped Bowden did not know all the facts, "because if he does, that's a very serious question of what's going on in sports." Bowden claimed his letter, which was introduced along with others at McDowell's sentencing, was meant to be private and had been misunderstood.

And he caused a stir when he came to the defense of University of Colorado football coach Gary Barnett, publicly questioning why alleged victims of rape by Colorado football players had delayed reporting it.

"I did not understand how a young lady can say she was abused, or whatever it was, two years later," Bowden said. "At the time, why don't you go report it? It seems like you ought to report it right [away]. So it makes me say, 'Well, did it really happen like that? I don't know.'"

Bowden found it easier to give the benefit of the doubt to players in trouble. His loyalty made him a beloved figure in the extended Seminoles family of current and former teammates. But with his willingness to dole out second chances came risks— and not a small amount of calculation that the athlete benefiting from Bowden's blessing would return the favor with a winning performance on the field. The obvious self-interest notwithstanding, Bowden preferred to frame it as a Christian obligation.

"I knew there were thousands of lost boys on the streets," he said. "I knew it was my job to help as many as I could."

In one of several inspirational books he coauthored about coaching, Bowden cited the example of Darnell Dockett, a troubled kid who found his own mother, a drug abuser, murdered when he was thirteen. Bowden signed Dockett to play defensive tackle, but he "had some problems" while at FSU, as Bowden cryptically described it, although he overcame them and went on to the pros. Not mentioned in Bowden's moving tribute was that while on the team, Dockett was arrested in 2003 for grand theft, a felony punishable by up to five years in prison; he avoided jail time with a plea bargain.

That same year, Bowden's quarterback, Adrian McPherson, was charged with theft and implicated in organized gambling; he was sentenced to thirty months' probation. The McPherson case led to the unprecedented spectacle of Bowden being called to testify at trial. In a moment that encapsulated the solicitous attitude toward the coaching legend among authorities in Tallahassee, the prosecutor joked to the judge before starting her questioning, "I don't have any questions, but I want to be able to say I cross-examined Coach Bowden."

Also in 2003, another of Bowden's players went on trial for sexual assault and was acquitted. And the quarterback was suspended and had to sit out the Sugar Bowl for skipping a final exam. Things were so bad that the university's athletic director at the time, Dave Hart, conceded that critics were right to raise concerns about how players were being recruited.

"That's an obvious question when you have these kind of problems," he said.

And the questions didn't just stop at Bowden's doorstep. T. K. Wetherell had just become president of Florida State when Bowden sent his letter on behalf of Ashley Witherspoon's rapist, Michael Gibson. Wetherell and Bowden went way back; Wetherell

had been a wide receiver on the football team when Bowden was
an assistant coach in the 1960s.

After Bowden's action on behalf of Gibson became public, the
National Organization for Women chapter in Florida sent an
angry letter to Wetherell saying the coach should be disciplined:
"Until FSU starts taking seriously sexual violence against women
by athletes, the school will continue to send the despicable message to hundreds of young men that rape is okay. Censuring
Bowden would be a good first indication of change of course."

Wetherell would have none of it. He issued a statement of support for Bowden.

"I have known Coach Bowden for years," Wetherell said. "I am
sure he never meant to suggest in any way that he condones any
type of abusive behavior."

T. K. Wetherell's dedication to Seminoles football could seem, at
times, over the top. Consider his performance at a Florida State
press conference in 2009, when he fell into a rambling diatribe
that sounded more akin to a wound-up head coach than a university president:

> Now, we understand all the rest of it. We've heard [colum-
> nist Mike] Bianchi over there saying, well hell, thirty-one
> wins don't count anyway because they were at some dipshit
> school . . .
>
>   I mean, I figured out how to beat Florida. I told them
> the other day—I've got the deal, man. I got the deal.
> We're going to send a graduate assistant down to write a
> [paper] for [Tim] Tebow, and go ahead and turn it in. And

then we're not going to tell anybody, until about the 15th of August. And we're going to say, "Oh, by the way, look what happened." Urban [Meyer] doesn't know anything about this—he's not involved. And the letter according to the NCAA—you think a violation occurred, not that it did occur, you think it occurred, you've got to sit him.

Well, we've got the proof, we've the [paper], we've got the one he turned in, we've got the one the graduate assistant [did]. He violated the rules. He's ineligible . . . now, they can redshirt him next year, and they may need to do that because they're going to need a quarterback, anyway, in two years and that may not be a bad idea. But—that's just not right. I mean, it's just not right. That's what's the problem— it's just flat wrong. . . .

At that point, a university spokesman rose from his chair and ended the press conference before it got any more embarrassing. Wetherell had been spouting off about penalties imposed on his school over the 2007 "*Apollo 13*" academic scandal in which tutors helped student athletes cheat on tests and wrote papers for them. Apoplectic over the NCAA's decision to take away twelve victories from football coach Bobby Bowden, Florida State's president made an ass of himself in front of the press and later had to apologize to the "dipshit school" he belittled.

While it may not be completely surprising in Wetherell's case—a colorful character who had a reputation for blunt talk— it nevertheless is instructive for what it says about misplaced priorities at the highest levels of some universities. Here, the head of one of the largest public institutions of higher education in the country went off the rails because his teams had a few wins taken away due to academic cheating.

One of the things weighing on Wetherell was the impact of the NCAA penalties on Bowden's record of career wins. After surpassing Joe Paterno in 2003, Bowden would remain ahead for several years until Paterno again caught up and edged into the lead. At the time of the NCAA's announcement, Paterno had 383 wins and Bowden had 382. Vacating those twelve wins was devastating. Bowden, never one to dwell publicly on the importance of his competition with Paterno, sounded uncharacteristically agitated following the NCAA's decision.

"Will I ever catch him?" he said of Paterno. "I don't know. But I'd like to have a shot. It would be nice for my grandkids. It would be nice for my children."

As fate would have it, time had run out for Bowden. Wetherell may have come to the defense of his coach—he instructed the university to challenge the NCAA's penalty—but he had made up his mind to cut him loose. The Seminoles were coming off a 7–6 season, the latest in a string of mediocre years—they hadn't won more than nine games since 2003—and boosters, fans, and university officials were restless. Bowden himself said later that after the 2009 season closed with a thumping loss to the hated Gators, "I thought to myself, 'My goose is cooked.'" The university had struck a deal in 2007 with his assistant, Jimbo Fisher, that would have required Florida State to pay Fisher $5 million if he wasn't named head coach by 2011.

The end came when Wetherell made a visit to Bowden's office, telling his old coach, "Bobby, this isn't going to be pretty." Wetherell said he had two options, the first being that Bowden could remain one more year as a sort of "ambassador coach" while Fisher actually called all the shots.

"Do you mean I'm the head coach, but can't go on the field?" Bowden asked.

"Yes," Wetherell said.

"Well, that option is out. What is the other option?"

"The other option is that we won't renew your contract."

Bowden chose the high road, resigning after thirty-four years at the helm of the Florida State football team. At age eighty, his quest for the title of winningest coach had ended.

On a cold, snowy Saturday in October 2011, Joe Paterno achieved a lifelong dream. A three-yard touchdown run with 1:08 left won the game for Penn State and handed him his 409th career win—making him the all-time winningest coach in NCAA Division I history, living or dead. Electronic signboards flashed congratulations to the eighty-four-year-old Paterno. Penn State president Graham Spanier presented him with a plaque with the inscription, "Joe Paterno, Educator of Men."

Two weeks later, both of them would be fired. And two months after that, Paterno would be dead.

The staggering downfall of one of the greatest coaches in the history of college sports was as swift as it was disturbing. Paterno's assistant, Jerry Sandusky, was finally charged in November 2011 with forty-five criminal counts involving sexual assaults on ten boys. When the full measure of Sandusky's monstrous crimes, and the university's failure to act on them, became known, people were horrified. So was Penn State's board of trustees, which had been kept in the dark for years by Spanier. Some trustees questioned why top officials, including Paterno, didn't do more to stop Sandusky when they had the chance. One of them noted that he had been shocked to see Sandusky at the Nittany Lion Club just weeks before he and two top university officials were indicted, given what Spanier and Paterno had known about the ongoing investigation.

Paterno claimed he had done all he could back in 2001 by forwarding the report of Sandusky's shower incident to the athletic director, and he denied knowing the full details of what happened to the boy. "If this is true we were all fooled, along with scores of professionals trained in such things, and we grieve for the victims and their families."

The public didn't buy it, and pressure built to do something about Paterno. He announced he intended to resign at the end of the season, but the board decided not to wait that long. It had an athletic department aide deliver a note to Paterno's home with a phone number to call. When he dialed it, he was informed he was being fired. Shaken, Paterno hung up. His wife picked up the phone and called back, berating the board for their treatment of her husband. When Paterno met with his coaches the next day, he broke down and sobbed.

Paterno died of cancer in January 2012, and it spared him what might have been the only thing worse than being terminated from Penn State: the NCAA's decision six months later to vacate all of his 112 wins dating back to 1998 and fine Penn State $60 million. Erasing his victories from the record books elevated Bobby Bowden and his 377 wins back to the top spot.

"I didn't want it to happen like this," a subdued Bowden said.

As the sun set on Bobby Bowden's long career, there was an outpouring of testimonials. One of them came from Francis "Monk" Bonasorte,* the former Florida State football star who had

---

*Bonasorte died in November 2016.

received a letter of support from his old coach at his sentencing for a drug conviction in 1987.

Bonasorte was a big believer in the Bowden way—not surprising, since he was a beneficiary of it. After his incarceration, Bonasorte had written to Bowden seeking guidance, and the coach wrote him back, saying, "I love you as much now as I ever did" and pledging to help Bonasorte "get started again." Bowden helped him land a job running the Florida State University Varsity Club, a position Bonasorte kept for thirteen years.

In one of several hagiographies published about Bowden as retirement neared, a grateful Bonasorte acknowledged that Bowden's willingness to make allowances for problematic players had hurt his reputation.

"People criticize him because he's had players not do the right things," Bonasorte said. "And he has also been criticized for how he disciplines those players—his three strikes rule. If after one mistake, a player is thrown to the wolves, what are his chances in life? I believe if you throw away that person after one mistake, his chances of being successful in life go down the drain."

Bonasorte also spoke of how college sports had become less forgiving since the days when Bowden gave him his big break by letting him join the team and supported him when he landed in hot water.

"I think the difference now is that the game has changed. It's a business," he said, adding that "everything is being watched. We got into trouble, and when we did, the coaches would have us get up and run at five o'clock in the morning. I spent a lot of time at the county line, running back to the campus with some coach driving behind me and my roommates. It was far. If you have kids, and they get into trouble, you don't tell the world. And that's the way it was back then."

Monk Bonasorte would eventually leave the Varsity Club to

join the administrative staff at Florida State's athletic department, where he rose to become senior associate athletics director, essentially the No. 2 position there. Bonasorte's office would
become a powerful post from which to carry on his mentor's
philosophy of giving football players in trouble a second chance.

FAMOUS JAMEIS

The little house on 25th Avenue North in Hueytown, Alabama, was a shrine to its biggest, brightest, and most celebrated occupant. Framed news clippings, photos, and awards attesting to his greatness adorned the living room walls. Well-wishers stopped by to show their respect.

If the living room was a shrine, the bedroom where the Great One grew up was practically a curated museum, each wall devoted to memorabilia from different stages in his development. Once, while feeling bored, he amused himself by narrating a brief cell phone video of what he called the "Boom Boom Room," panning the camera from one wall to the next, beginning with his formative days in elementary school in nearby Bessemer.

"Know how it started off? Started off with those Bessemer boys, showing all them championships," he said, lingering on a wall adorned with a jacket bearing his name, surrounded by photos of himself. Then it was on to "the basketball wall" before panning "over here to the football wall, you know what it is, got my little stand over there . . . got my little man on top of the window . . . there go my graduation suit . . . my little idols when I was coming up." There were lots of trophies—Gatorade State Player of the

Year, Under Armour All-America Game MVP—news clippings, ribbons, jerseys with his name on them.

He wasn't done yet. The video continued to a corner of the room decorated with honors he got in middle school from a sporting goods store in Alabama called Hibbetts that recognized outstanding young athletes. "On over here to the Hibbett Sports. You know, I was a superstar when I was a little kid too."

Finally, there was also an academic wall, festooned with certificates and honors. Because the Great One was exceptionally bright, if a little self-conscious about it. For this part of the narration, his down-homey drawl suddenly took on a pinched, faux-erudite defensiveness.

"To those who believe that I am dumb, let me please reiterate the academic wall, where I have made straight As," he intoned, before signing off testily: "Thank you, have a nice day."

Yes, Jameis Winston was the full package. The archetypical "student-athlete" that college sports overlords lusted after, he seemed to validate the increasingly strained notion that it was possible to excel at sports and still do well academically. A big kid with a great throwing arm and a winning personality, "Famous Jameis" had been the hero of Hueytown High, a multisport phenom who was as good on the baseball diamond as he was at quarterback.

A crush of college coaches pursued him when it was time to graduate from high school. At Florida State, Jimbo Fisher had recently taken over as head football coach from the retiring Bobby Bowden, and was determined to make his mark by landing Winston and a handful of other star recruits. For Fisher, a lot was on the line.

Under Bowden, he had basically been a coach-in-waiting, promised the top job one day, and now that he had it, the pressure was on to deliver. He had a good first season in 2010, taking the team to a 10–4 record, the first time in seven years it had won more than nine games. But 2011 was disappointing, and now he was expected to turn things around with more permanence.

One way to do that was to recruit the best high school players he could find, and Fisher went at it with a vengeance. His aggressive pursuit of several top Alabama athletes caused a stir in that state, where the head coach of the fearsome Crimson Tide, Nick Saban, had once been Fisher's boss. Speaking at a football club event in Montgomery, Fisher was unapologetic.

"Hey, college football is tough. It's tough to get to the top and it's hard to stay there," he said. "Right here in this state, you have the last three national champions. We know what we're going against. But we have a great product to sell, too. Florida State has been a national program since Bobby Bowden built it into what it is. It's a national brand. We're not hoping to compete at the elite level. We expect it and demand it of ourselves."

For his part, Winston, too, wanted to stake his claim to greatness, and he was keeping his options open. He was viewed as equally talented at football and baseball, and when he decided to accept Fisher's pitch to come to the Seminoles, part of the deal was he'd also play for the baseball team there. Signing with Florida State in 2012, he told ESPN he wasn't sure yet which sport he would pursue into the pros. But he had his criteria figured out.

"Honestly," he said, "money is probably the biggest factor in my decision."

Baseball may be America's national pastime, but it doesn't butter the bread at Florida State, so it wasn't long before Winston was told he needed to abandon his dream of being another double-sport Bo Jackson and concentrate on football. He was assumed to be headed eventually to the NFL—if he could just stay out of trouble while in school. That was proving harder than it should have been.

At Florida State, he was caught stealing crab legs from a local grocery store and had to perform community service. A Burger King employee called the cops on Winston after he ignored her repeated requests to stop taking soda without paying for it. And he was suspended for standing on a table in front of students and, repeating a crude Internet meme, yelling, "Fuck her right in the pussy!"

Comments by his father following the crab-legs incident revealed an unsettling sense of entitlement, if not denial. Antonor Winston suggested that others had let his son down as he struggled with his growing celebrity.

"I think it should show the university and us, I think we probably kind of dropped the ball on that a little bit," he said, adding, "He's supposed to have somebody around him 24/7."

In fact, Jameis Winston had barely arrived on campus as a freshman in the fall of 2012 when troubling signs emerged. At some point during that winter, Winston got to know a medical student at Florida State in her early twenties. The young woman, who came from a culturally conservative family, had not slept with Winston, though she regarded him as a friend—she made him cupcakes for his birthday.

One night, she got a call from Winston asking if she could come pick up him and some other football players at a bar. The woman returned with Winston to his apartment, where they had a sexual encounter. He said it was consensual. However, the circumstances of it would lead her to seek counseling from the resident advisor in her dormitory, who reported it to the university victim's advocate office. The woman did not call it rape. But the interlude with Winston "was of such a nature that she felt violated or felt that she needed to seek some type of counseling for her emotions about the experience," a prosecutor said later.

It was perhaps an early insight into how Winston viewed

women. He would later testify in a legal deposition that, by his own estimate, he may have had fifty or more sexual partners during his first years at Florida State, did not remember their names, and rarely saw any of them more than once.

"I didn't date any of those girls," he said.

Winston added that he and his teammate Chris Casher, a close friend and roommate who was also from Alabama, would watch each other have sex, saying it was "kind of like real live porn." For his part, Casher said the two of them would sometimes try to both have sex with the same girls they picked up at clubs, explaining that "it's kind of a football player thing" that they did.

"We can kind of, like, run 'em," Casher said, "that is kind of how we do it."

Ironically, it wasn't his sexual activities that first landed Winston in hot water. A few months into his freshman year, he and Casher were stopped at gunpoint and handcuffed by university police after someone reported seeing two men walking on a trail and brandishing a firearm. The two football players said they were using the realistic-looking pellet pistol to shoot squirrels. They were let go.

Winston and Casher returned to their apartment that day at Legacy Suites, a privately run complex near campus where Florida State athletics housed freshman football players. It was one of the perks of being a college athlete. While freshman students at many public universities can expect to be sandwiched into a blocky dorm room with two or three roommates, that's usually not the case if they are in a sport that is important to the school. Student-athletes are often sequestered in their own residences, have access to special food services, and generally are treated better. At Legacy Suites, Winston and other young members of the football team all seemed to have motor scooters (older players had cars), even though it was unclear how some could afford them.

One of the drawbacks of clustering freshman athletes together outside the normal student housing system is that they are not always supervised. After getting back to Legacy Suites on the day of the squirrel-shooting incident, Winston, Casher, and other team members got into a sprawling battle at their apartment complex with BB guns, pellet pistols, and paintballs. The mayhem had been going on, intermittently, for a month, and caused more than $4,000 in broken windows and damaged walls and appliances. That night, the apartment manager, David Sudekum, had had enough. He contacted the Florida State coaching staff, but didn't get much of a response. So he called the police. What happened next is typical of the way many criminal incidents involving college athletes play out.

Sudekum told officers he planned to evict the football players and wanted them to cover the cost of repairs. Because the damage exceeded $1,000, the case was being investigated as a potential felony. That was a problem for Florida State, because under its rules, any athlete who faced a felony charge was automatically suspended from the team.

But the athletic department had a guy who knew how to work the system to keep players out of trouble. He was the main point of contact for the police whenever they needed to talk to a player, he was in touch with lawyers, and he generally cleaned up messes.

His name was Monk Bonasorte, the associate athletic director and protégé of Bobby Bowden.

Officers reached out to Bonasorte to "schedule interviews" with two of the football players implicated in the vandalism, according to a police report of the incident. Afterwards, an officer wrote: "Mr. Bonasorte explained that most of the additional players involved had been contacted and it was determined that the cost of the repair would be divided equally among all players. Mr. Bonasorte had been in contact with Mr. Sudekum to inform him that the damages would be paid. I received a message from Mr. Sudekum stating that he was certain that he did not want to pursue charges."

It was all cleaned up.

Granted, the incident was hardly a federal offense. And there's something to be said for giving a break once in a while to young people who can be prone to stupid mischief. But here, it wasn't so simple. This was at least the second encounter with police for Winston, and the third for Casher—he had been implicated in yet another incident in which BBs were shot from a car at pedestrians on the street, one that had also led to no charges being filed.

If some version of the "broken windows" theory of crime— little problems left unaddressed can lead to bigger ones—applies to college athletics, then it helps explain what unfolded on the night of December 6, 2012, less than two weeks after the Legacy Suites shootout.

At nineteen, Erica Kinsman wasn't legally able to obtain alcohol, but like a lot of college students who flocked to Potbelly's in downtown Tallahassee, she found a way, despite lacking the wristband the bar gives to patrons who meet the minimum drinking age. An older friend bought the alcohol that evening in December 2012. It was "Purgatory Thursday" at Potbelly's, meaning students could drink all they wanted for ten bucks.

A pretty blonde freshman looking to get on the pre-med track at Florida State, Erica seemed slightly out of her comfort zone as she shared mixed drinks with her friend Monique Kessler in the jostling bar, music thumping in the background. An odd little "Indian-looking" man had been following her around the bar, making her nervous. Then, a tall black guy pulled her aside and struck up a conversation. Eventually, he got around to asking for her phone number. Erica looked at Monique, not sure what to do.

"I mean, like, if you want to," Monique said.

Erica gave the guy her number. He tapped it into his cell phone, and Monique and Erica walked away. A couple of girls approached Erica and asked her if she was aware of who she had been talking to. She was not. His name was Chris, they said, the only freshman starting linebacker on the Florida State football team. Later, after sharing a few drinks and a shot during the evening with her friends, Erica got a text message from an unknown number:

meet me out front

"Should I go?" she asked Monique.

Erica went outside, where events began to take a turn for the worse. She got into a Yellow cab with "Chris" and two other guys, and somehow lost her driver's license in the process—it was found in the gutter outside Potbelly's the next day and returned to her. The cab driver thought she seemed drunk. Chris sat in the front and Erica in the back, next to one of his friends, a big guy with a poofy short Afro. Chris kept asking Erica if she could get in touch with Monique to come join them, but she never did. They arrived at Legacy Suites Apartments, and when it was time to pay the cab fare, all three young men pulled out FSU IDs in order to get a student discount. All of them then went up to an apartment Chris shared with the guy Erica had been sitting with in the cab.

The next thing Erica says she recalls is Chris's roommate forcing himself on her in his bedroom. She says she felt woozy and sick and tried to resist, but he held down her arms and legs. He told her it would be okay and to just let him finish. Suddenly his bedroom door opened and the third guy who had shared the cab ride to the apartment, a young man with long dreadlocks, stuck his head in, according to Erica.

"Dude," he said, "she's telling you to stop."

Then Chris came into the bedroom to see if he could join in, too. Told he could not, he took out his cell phone and started videotaping the sex. The guy with the dreadlocks told Chris, "You crazy," and left. That is when the guy having sex with Erica got up and carried her into the bathroom, locking the door behind him. She says he laid her down and resumed having sex, pushing her face to the tile floor. Then he was finished.

"Okay," he said, "you can leave now."

He offered to give her a ride back to her place on his scooter because she did not know where she was. She had him drop her off a short distance from her dorm near Stadium Drive, because she did not want him to know where she lived. Erica recalled that he would not face her and seemed to be trying to keep her from getting a close look at him.

By then, it was the early morning hours of December 7. Erica immediately started reaching out to friends for help. Monique Kessler got a text message from Erica saying:

come find me

Bria Henry also got a text:

please call me

Friends of Erica's on Twitter noticed tweets she was posting over and over again, pleading:

someone please call me

One of those friends, Jenna Weisberg, did. Erica, sounding hysterical, told her she thought she had been raped but could not remember everything. She was reluctant to call the police because she did not want anyone to be "mad at me." Jenna surmised Erica was afraid of her parents' reaction and didn't want the cops to discover her underage drinking. After convincing Erica she needed to report it, Jenna called 911 herself.

A police officer responded and drove Erica to Tallahassee Memorial Hospital. A nurse specializing in sexual assault cases noted fresh bruises above her left knee and on the right forearm, and redness on both knees and right foot. She also reported "vaginal tenderness," muscle aches, and nausea. A rape kit examination was performed. Erica's mother and father rushed to Tallahassee, arriving at the hospital at dawn to find their daughter sobbing and throwing up.

They crawled into her hospital bed, held Erica in their arms, and cried together.

Erica Kinsman didn't know the identity of the man she says raped her. She told everything she could remember to detectives with the Tallahassee Police Department in December 2012, and then waited. In the meantime, she tried to get back to her normal routine.

In January 2013, on the first day of a new semester, Erica took a seat in one of her classes. As other students filed in, she suddenly had a flash of recognition. There, settling into a desk not far from hers, was her alleged attacker. Composing herself, Erica listened as the professor called out students' names and eventually came around to him: Jameis Winston. Winston noticed Erica looking at him, and they held each other's gaze for a moment. She thought he looked concerned.

He needn't have been.

The police had been doing little to properly investigate Erica's complaint. Even though they had the name of Winston's roommate—Chris—and knew from Erica that he was a freshman on the football team, detectives had not gotten anywhere. Potbelly's had thirty security cameras that could have allowed them to easily identify who Erica left the bar with, but they never asked to review them. They failed to find the cab driver or locate a receipt for the credit card one of the men used to pay the fare.

Now, however, Erica had a name. She called Detective Scott Angulo, the lead investigator on her case, with this new information. He sent an email to his supervisors alerting them that she had identified Jameis Winston. Previously, he wrote, he had "no real leads," but Winston's physical description and living arrangements fit what Erica had originally reported to police. Angulo was careful to note in his email that Winston "is a FSU football player."

Erica said that given this new information, police detectives seemed less than eager to pursue the case. Angulo—one of the many cops who earned extra pay working side jobs at FSU football games—discouraged her, she said, telling one of her family members: "This is a huge football town. You should really think long and hard if you want to press charges." Inexplicably, rather than bringing Winston—now a rape suspect—in for questioning, police waited eleven days and then called him on his cell phone and asked to arrange a time to talk. Winston told them he had baseball practice and would call them back.

Then they telephoned Monk Bonasorte at the Florida State athletic department and told him Winston had been accused of sexual assault. Bonasorte sprang into action. Phone records show he made a series of calls in the next few hours to head football coach Jimbo Fisher, the Seminole Boosters, and a Tallahassee criminal defense lawyer, R. Timothy Jansen, who serves as a sort of guardian angel for Florida State football players in trouble. When the time came for Winston to appear for his scheduled interview with detectives the next day, he failed to show up. Instead, Jansen appeared and said Winston would not be speaking to them.

After that, the case was effectively shelved. Police did not pursue witnesses or DNA evidence. They did not discover that Chris Casher had actually recorded part of the sexual encounter between Jameis Winston and Erica Kinsman. Nor did Florida State University initiate its own investigation, as required under federal education laws. Instead, athletic officials decided, without talking to Erica or her attorney, and apparently without passing it on to administrators outside their department, that her complaint was without merit. Asked later why he had not told anyone outside the athletic department about the rape accusation, Fisher, who had been Bobby Bowden's assistant before succeeding him as head coach, said he was only obligated to report it to one person: Monk Bonasorte.

By spring, Winston appeared to have put the assault allegation behind him. He played in his first off-season practice game and stunned everybody, completing twelve of fifteen passes for two touchdowns and more than two hundred yards, a near-perfect performance for a rookie that had fans, sports writers, and TV talking heads singing his praises. Coach Fisher was asked how Winston was handling all the raised expectations.

He responded that Winston seemed to be doing okay. And then Fisher—one of the few people who knew about Erica Kinsman's complaint—made an observation packed with the kind of double meaning that can only be appreciated with the benefit of hindsight.

"But the guy's gonna stumble," he said. "Occasionally, he's going to make a mistake. Hopefully, we'll be talented enough around him to help in those moments."

EXCESSIVE
DEVOTION

INSANITY

D r. William Preston Few was the embodiment of a Southern gentleman.

An academic from Greenville County, South Carolina, he was soft-spoken and gracious. His father had studied medicine and was a surgeon in the Confederate Army. The young Dr. Few pursued a more gossamer path, getting his degree in modern languages at Harvard before decamping back to the South, where the temperate climate better suited his chronic ill health.

He was frail, bespectacled, and given to shyness. An acquaintance once wrote, after meeting him, that Dr. Few "had little to say and seemed not a very forceful man." But like many men of letters in his day, the first president of Duke University let his pen do the talking.

As dean of Duke's predecessor school, Trinity College, he prepared a report in 1903 affirming the principle of academic freedom, part of a successful effort to save the job of a professor who had ignited outrage by suggesting that the African-American Booker T. Washington was "the greatest man, save General Lee, born in the South in a hundred years." The courageous stand in the face of intolerance secured a reputation of integrity for

Dr. Few's school and hinted at a progressive spirit that danced behind his lively brown eyes.

Yet as 1906 dawned, Dr. Few was deeply troubled. The source of his unease wasn't a tenure dispute or some other rarefied concern of the academy that might be expected to occupy the thoughts of a college dean. It was football. The roughneck sport had taken hold in the late 1800s at the prestigious universities of the North and quickly spread south, bringing with it a reputation for injuries and deaths on the field, and, to his mind, a general air of disgrace.

Back then, crimes involving college football players were mostly confined to the playing field. At least eighteen players died and more than 150 were injured in 1905, and it was widely recognized that in the absence of strictly enforced codes of conduct, athletes were purposely kicked and stomped while down on the ground. The nature of the sport at that time—almost entirely a running game, where teams would grind out yards through bruising advances, with little or no protective gear—encouraged bloodshed. Ringers—non-students paid to play—were known to infiltrate teams, and other forms of cheating were rampant.

The state of affairs became so bad that President Theodore Roosevelt summoned the head coaches of Harvard, Princeton, and Yale to the White House to lecture them on the need to regulate football. Not that Teddy had any qualms about the inherent brutishness of the sport. "I believe in outdoor games," he said, "and I don't mind in the least that they are rough games, or that those who take part in them are occasionally injured.

"But," he warned, "when these injuries are inflicted by others, either wantonly or of set design, we are confronted by the question not of damage to one man's body, but of damage to the other man's character."

Dr. Few shared the concern, and he knew of which he spoke.

Despite his lack of athleticism, one of his duties upon joining Trinity was "manager of athletics." This was not uncommon in an era when sports were still ancillary pastimes at most campuses and professors volunteered to serve as coaches. At Dr. Few's Trinity, the founding football coach in 1888 was an academic who had studied economics at Yale and Dartmouth.

But for Dr. Few, the concern went beyond just injuries on the field. He saw bigger dangers ahead, a dark thunderhead on the horizon of higher education in his beloved South. At the dawn of the twentieth century, the post–Civil War South was still emerging from Reconstruction. Universities, long settled and thriving in the North, were only then coming into their own in Southern states, after years of war and impoverishment. Sports programs at Southern colleges had not yet achieved the status or success of their Northern peers—but oh, how they wanted to. Once they had a taste of it, colleges in the South wasted little time pushing to make their football programs bigger and better.

The first football coach at what would become Florida State University in 1902 was a professor of Latin named W. W. Hughes. Within two seasons he was replaced by a player-coach, Jack "Pee Wee" Forsythe, reflecting the growing presence of professional coaches on college football squads. Already, tension was brewing between the competing priorities of academics and sports. As Hughes's final season drew to a close, Florida State's Platonic and Anaxagorean Debating Societies held a hotly contested debate with members of the athletic department on the topic of whether "debating societies are more beneficial to colleges than football teams."

There was little doubt about where Pee Wee Forsythe stood. The coach had little use for "the arm chair football critic" wringing his hands over violence on the field or the undermining of academic values.

"How often this year have we seen in our newspapers, lurid appeals to the Legislature and college authorities to stop a sport, that to note their tone, you would imagine was as dangerous as a Boer regiment or Japanese squadron?" he said. "Legislation! What has a Legislature to do with a college boy's sport?"

Forysthe spoke for many when he extolled the virtues of football as a new type of ambassador for a college or university, an activity where fast-paced action, the thrill of competition, and fan loyalty came together to project a positive image. Where Florida boys had played, he said, they had left the impression of gentlemen.

"To a young and growing university like this, nothing could be or is of more value as an advertising agency than its football teams—an advertisement in its best sense."

From his ivy-entwined perch in North Carolina, Dr. Few surveyed the same college sports landscape with trepidation. He looked at the mayhem up north and worried that the "exaggerated emphasis put upon intercollegiate athletics" was endangering the noble ideals of higher education. Taking up his pen as 1905 drew to a close, he set about writing a commentary for the *South Atlantic Quarterly,* the same journal that had published the incendiary comments of the Trinity professor comparing Booker T. Washington to Robert E. Lee several years earlier. The title of Dr. Few's essay was "The Excessive Devotion to Athletics."

He acknowledged the difficulty of having a rational discussion about it.

"We in the South are justly proud of the sense of honor and spirit of chivalry that manifest themselves in so many phases of the life of this gentle and generous people," he wrote. "By some strange perversity, men honorable to the minutest detail of conduct in all other matters, in this one thing become sophisticated and unwilling to meet issues squarely."

Nevertheless, he plowed ahead. A devout Methodist, Dr. Few tended to frame things in terms of good and evil. He drew a connection between the "evils and dangers in college sports and the evils and dangers in the business world.

"The intensity with which college sports are pursued is a manifestation of the spirit which the American people put into everything. And the craze for winning games embodies the spirit and methods of trade."

Money, he believed, was at the root of this particular rot spreading like a canker in the groves of academe.

"These evils are more pronounced in the larger and older colleges of the East and North. They are evils that have grown out of mere bigness. They have come from great prosperity, like many of the evils in the business and political life of the country," he wrote, suggesting that "perhaps to abolish the gate receipts" from the sale of game tickets would help by removing the incentive of profit.

Finally, he fretted over what was to become of Southern schools as the march toward football parity with the North surged ahead. The state of education in the South was still disorganized, and college communities "too sparsely settled to give Southern intercollegiate games the vast crowds and immense gate receipts that have produced fanaticism and wild enthusiasm in the North."

But the South was growing rapidly and pressure was building to better organize the scrambled patchwork of higher-education institutions. Therefore, it was "absolutely essential that all reputable Southern colleges at once put themselves right" in the matter of football.

"Prosperity will soon come to intercollegiate athletics," he warned, "and if to the evils of disorganization we add the evils that come from bigness and prosperity, we shall have a state of things that will be unendurable."

The National Collegiate Athletic Association had a problem. There was a growing sense that college sports had run amok, with players being recruited with cash, gamblers betting on games, and a general sense that the corrupting influence of money had inspired an existential crisis. There were calls for reform.

The setting was a conference of NCAA members in July 1946. Dr. Few was gone, having dropped dead six years earlier at age seventy-two while still serving as president of Duke. He had lived long enough to see his fears about college football realized, yet passed from the scene before he could witness the surprisingly strong response that emerged from the conference members who met to decide how to fix the problem.

The response was called the "Sanity Code." It was actually the second major reform effort, the first being the turn-of-the-century threat by President Roosevelt to ban the rampantly violent sport of football from campuses, which had spawned the precursor to the NCAA. But the Sanity Code went further, taking aim directly at the influence of money. It barred the recruitment of athletes with promises of financial aid and required that they be held to the same academic standards as any other student. The penalty for violators was expulsion from the NCAA.

Alas, by 1950, college sports' brief dalliance with sanity was over. "The restrictions in the Sanity Code were such that the majority of institutions felt they couldn't live by it," an NCAA official said later. Much of the opposition came from public universities in the South.

What happened next would help lay the foundation for the commercial edifice of college athletics in the modern era. A new set of guidelines emerged that permitted the awarding of financial "grants-in-aid" to prospective players, who came to be referred to as "student-athletes," a term coined by then-NCAA president Walter Byers that cast a patina of amateurism over the program. That amateur ideal would become enshrined in court opinions denying compensation—and injury or death benefits— for college players and their families for decades to come.

In overturning a lower court's grant of benefits to the wife and three children of Ray Dennison, a college football player killed on the gridiron in 1955, the Colorado Supreme Court found that Fort Lewis A&M "was not in the football business" and therefore its dead athlete was not an employee entitled to benefits. "In fact," the justices wrote, "the state conducted institution, supported by taxpayers, could not as a matter of business enter into the maintenance of a football team for the purpose of making a profit directly or indirectly out of the taxpayers' money."

The Colorado justices, without a sense of irony, had put their finger on a fundamental paradox of commercialized college sports: public universities cannot legally run a for-profit sports program, at least without paying taxes on it. For that matter, neither can private nonprofit schools like Stanford and Notre Dame.

In fact, at mid-century, taxation of commercial enterprises run by colleges was becoming a controversial political issue that went beyond athletics. New York University's attempt to extend its tax-exempt status to profits generated by C.F. Mueller Company, a pasta maker donated to the law school in 1947, was one of the more outlandish examples of universities skirting taxes on commercial operations that had little to do with education. By the 1950s, growing concern over the practice spawned the Unrelated Business Income Tax, which targeted activities deemed tangential to a nonprofit organization's tax-exempt mission.

In debating these issues, Congress heard from defenders of college athletics, notably the NCAA, which seemed to have abandoned its previous charge up the hill toward sanity and now was embarked on a path to commercialism. It wanted to ensure that the new tax would not ensnare revenue from the increasingly sophisticated sports programs run by many schools. House and Senate committee reports in 1950 declared that "athletic activities of schools are substantially related to their educational functions," even specifying football and basketball as examples of this tax-exempt educational benefit.

But by 1977, the Internal Revenue Service was looking at the burgeoning television revenue from college games and asking why it should not be a taxable unrelated business. When word of the agency's reconsideration got out, colleges and the NCAA furiously lobbied lawmakers and top IRS officials against it. Sheldon Cohen, a former IRS commissioner under President Johnson whom a group of colleges retained in their fight, recalled making the argument that despite its financial success, college athletics remained "related to the education function."

"That was the thought, that it's an adjunct to the schools but it's still school-based," said Cohen.

The IRS backed off, concluding that broadcasting games to television viewers was not that different from selling tickets to the local fans, students, and alumni who go to the school stadium. The agency has not publicly revisited the issue since. Looking at the landscape of college sports today, Cohen said he believes the tax exemption is still mostly valid, though harder to defend.

"People have taken the license you gave for a smaller operation and taken it into the big leagues," he said. "A difference in degree is a difference in kind."

And the difference in degree is staggering.

The frayed mill town of Bristol, Connecticut, like many small communities, is proud of the handful of big things it has. Framed pictures of them hang on the walls of the Friendly's restaurant on Route 6. There's the Otis Elevator testing tower, a sort of mini-skyscraper looming incongruously above the treetops. There's Lake Compounce, the oldest continuously operating amusement park in the country.

And then there's ESPN. Festooned with gigantic satellite arrays, the headquarters of the world's biggest broadcaster of sports programming resembles a moon base in the middle of a farmer's field. It took root in Bristol by chance in the late 1970s, when a former TV sports director, Bill Rasmussen, was looking for a cheap way to televise games of the old Hartford Whalers hockey team and University of Connecticut basketball. Called the Entertainment and Sports Programming Network, its first twenty-four-hour cable sports show, *SportsCenter*, aired on September 7, 1979.

From the beginning, ESPN had its core audience pegged: college sports fans. That very first broadcast featured host Lee Leonard, sporting '70s-era helmet hair, fat necktie, and eyeglasses that resembled ski goggles, declaring that "as of now" the sports universe had relocated to Bristol, Connecticut.

"And we're just minutes away from the first event on the ESPN schedule," he said. "That's the 1979 NCAA college football preview."

What started with much skepticism soon became a media behemoth, straddling college and professional sports and setting much of the business agenda for both industries. The staggering growth in money and clout for ESPN, and college sports in general, can be seen in the fees commanded for broadcasting games in the Big East Conference, of which UConn basketball was a member at the time of ESPN's founding. In 1979, the Big East was paid $305,000 for broadcast rights; thirty-two years later, ESPN would offer $100 million for those rights.

Schools trip over themselves hoping to attract ESPN's College Game Day, a roving festival of marketing, corporate sponsorships, and fan mania that picks different university campuses from which to broadcast an all-day promotional run-up to a game. Universities also allow ESPN a say in scheduling games and choosing matchups. ESPN's decision to air more college games during the week led to some schools volunteering to play, hoping for a bigger share of the television revenue pie but also opening themselves to criticism that weekday games interfere with studying by athletes and disrupt the academic atmosphere.

ESPN appears unconcerned. College sports is one of the biggest moneymakers for the company, which has a market value exceeding $50 billion and is now owned by Walt Disney and Hearst Corporation. If anything, ESPN has doubled down on intercollegiate athletics. In 2012, it struck a twelve-year deal worth $5.6 billion to broadcast college football playoffs. The universities share in those profits, most of it tax-free.

Richard Schmalbeck, a Duke University law professor who specializes in tax matters, said the IRS in the 1970s did not foresee the commercialized powerhouse that college sports would become, driven by national television viewership and the pioneering broadcast strategies of ESPN.

"Their reasoning was probably wrong at the time, but they were thinking not much was at stake because these numbers were pretty small and involved mostly local broadcasts," Schmalbeck said. "But if you're talking about ESPN Game Day, you're reaching an audience today that is fundamentally different than the audience who is at the event."

By 2013, schools in the NCAA's Division I were taking in a total of $8 billion in sports revenue. As the numbers have swelled, a whole profit-driven infrastructure has built up to support and expand it.

At Florida State—where sports generated $50 million in 2015 from broadcast rights and sponsorships, and another $25 million in ticket sales—money comes in through something called Seminole IMG College, the marketing arm of the athletic department. It's run by a private for-profit company, IMG, which controls the university's "athletically related radio broadcasts, coaches' TV shows, coaches' endorsements, game programs, ticket sales, corporate sponsorships and hospitality, internet sales and promotions."

IMG, whose employees have an office on campus, is a marketing giant that stands astride the college sports industry, representing more than two hundred of what it calls "the nation's top collegiate properties," including the NCAA and several conferences. IMG is among a handful of major players that comprise a sort of "corporate-athletics complex," seamlessly integrated into the athletic departments of major universities. Perhaps more than anything else, their presence signifies college sports' transformation from an amateur pursuit into a thoroughly commercial endeavor.

"It's sort of a fraud to be labeling it an educational enterprise," said John Colombo, a University of Illinois law professor who has studied the finances of college sports. "It's no different than if a university opened a BMW dealership and called it part of the educational enterprise."

With the threat of a multibillion-dollar tax bill hinging on the illusion that big-time college sports is merely a nonprofit educational pursuit, maintaining the facade of amateurism became critically important. And that meant, first and foremost, denying student athletes the right to profit from their talents.

This imperative gave rise to an Orwellian regulatory regime enforced by the NCAA, wherein "gifts" worth even a few dollars are prohibited; the University of Oregon was once found in violation after its athletic department gave shaving supplies to a football recruit who had left his razor at home. Indeed, one of the biggest obstacles to reforming collegiate athletics, ironically, has been the NCAA's insistence on treating college players as amateurs whose participation in sports is akin to an extracurricular activity, rather than a vocation. This, despite its acknowledgment that college athletics, at least at the Division I level, had long ago lost any semblance of amateurism.

In an internal memo from 2008, Myles Brand, the NCAA's president, noted how big-time college sports had turned into a race for cash and that some universities were pushing the envelope to find ways to finance it through "aggressive commercial activity and media exposure." Bad things were happening "for monetary reasons," he said, including: "(1) scheduling games that satisfy TV's needs but interfere with student-athlete academic time; (2) venues become crowded with commercialism in a way that is unbecoming to a university environment; and (3) student-athletes are promoted—exploited—to celebrity status in order to build fan and media interest."

Brand went on to fret that "the growth rate of athletic expenditures has caught the attention of Congress" and that, in an era of rising tuition rates, there would be pressure to reduce college spending on sports. The "worst-case" scenario, he said, would be a push to eliminate the tax-exempt status of intercollegiate athletics.

Although universities were resigned to embracing commercialism to help pay for athletics, he said, "there are some obvious limitations to commercial activity in college sports."

"The line in the sand," Brand stated, "is that student athletes should not be remunerated."

It's clear that the athletes themselves see through the hypocrisy. Several of them filed lawsuits against the NCAA over their inability to profit from their sport, arguing that its obvious for-profit nature belied the schools' insistence that it was all about education.

"Games are festooned with the names and logos of corporate sponsors and stadia in which games are telecast bear corporate names, all of which are captured by the cameras during broadcasts. Advertisements appear on sideline banners, physically painted on football fields and basketball courts, and digitally embedded into broadcasts," one lawsuit said. "Additionally, student athletes are often human billboards bearing corporate logos on their uniforms."

In a deposition for the NCAA litigation, former NBA star Tate George, a University of Connecticut alum, was asked if paying student athletes "would make college basketball the same as professional basketball."

"It's pretty much that now," George said, adding, "The universities are built on the sports programs, so a lot of the kids go there because of, you know, the recognition of athletes in the sporting world."

As for himself, "I went to UConn because of the conference, not because of the education."

Collegiate athletic officials, meanwhile, secretly worry about the ramifications of the monster they created. In 2010, a senior NCAA official, Wallace Renfro, sat at his computer and wrote an email to the NCAA president in which he bullet-pointed some pressing issues, including "criminal behavior" by student athletes. Renfro said, somewhat presciently, that "the most immediate focus is on relationship or domestic violence" and they needed a plan for addressing it.

"Often, but not always, there is an association between the lack of social responsibility and the abuse of drugs or alcohol that fuels the hubris of elite athletic status," he opined.

Ticking off a long list of concerns—"commercial exploitation," "corporate partners," "academic success"—Renfro groped for solutions, including possibly rethinking the old "student athlete" ruse.

"Maybe," he said, "we don't call them student-athletes any longer and just refer to them as students."

BIGNESS AND PROSPERITY

When Florida State University's board of trustees gathered on a late spring afternoon in 2013 to discuss the criteria for hiring a new athletic director, bigness and prosperity were in the air. The trustees wanted more of both.

The starting quarterback of the university's football team, Jameis Winston, had been accused of rape, but the trustees didn't know it yet, thanks to the athletic department keeping a lid on that disturbing information. What the board did know was that it had been more than a decade since the team won a national title, and Florida State had been throwing resources into its sports program ever since. The athletic department budget had ballooned from about $20 million to $90 million over the previous twenty years, and there were plans in the works for $80 million in improvements to the football stadium that houses Bobby Bowden Field. The school's priorities were reflected in its checkbook: while academic spending per student had increased about 40 percent in the ten years preceding 2013, football spending per player had shot up more than 100 percent.

The trustees took their seats around a modern U-shaped table in the Augustus B. Turnbull III Conference Center, named for the late provost and academician known for his dedication to the humanities. Among the trustees present was the chairman, Allan Bense, a former speaker of the Florida state house and a consultant to companies involved in road building, insurance, and golf courses. Also seated there was trustee Ed Burr, a real estate developer and a director of the Seminole Boosters, the powerful private group that supports Florida State University athletics.

Continuing around the table, the Seminole Boosters were also represented by Joe Camps, a doctor and former captain of the Florida State football team who once served as the group's chairman; Mark Hillis, a lawyer and banker who was a member of the Boosters; Les Pantin, a public relations executive, Seminole Boosters board member, and past chairman of Miami's Orange Bowl Committee, host to college football's national championship game; and attorney Andy Haggard, a former Boosters chairman, Orange Bowl Committee member, and inductee into the FSU Athletics Hall of Fame.

Then there was Susie Busch-Transou, a member of the Anheuser-Busch family who spearheaded an Anheuser-Busch-sponsored drinking event in Tallahassee, called Downtown Getdown, to coincide with Florida State football tailgate parties; Peggy Rolando, a real estate lawyer specializing in condominiums, hotels, and resorts; accountant Joe Gruters, a Republican Party operative, former vice president of Yacht Clubs of the Americas, and board member of the Florida Sports Foundation; Brent Sembler, a shopping center developer and political fundraiser; and June Duda, a member of a Florida family that runs a large real estate and farm management company.

Rounding out the group of trustees were two token members: a representative of the Florida State faculty, a computer science professor named Gary Tyson, and a student, Rosie Contreras.

When it came time to discuss qualifications for the new athletic director, June Duda spoke first.

"I would want to see a CEO, businessperson type," she said. "I don't want a former coach. I want somebody interested in the business of athletics."

Joe Gruters picked up on that theme. Florida State should follow the University of Michigan's example of hiring a former chief executive of Domino's Pizza to run its athletic department, he said.

"It's all business-oriented, it's about driving the revenues," said Gruters, adding that "in terms of raising revenue dollars," it was important that the new director focus on creating a more competitive football schedule.

"The schedule in football is going to be essential," agreed Les Pantin. "Beginning next season, when we go from the BCS to the college football playoffs, the schedule is going to be essential."

Susie Busch-Transou gave a nod to academics. She reminded the board of its goal to catch up to its peers and break into the ranks of the top twenty-five public colleges nationwide, something that had long eluded FSU, despite Florida having the fourth-largest economy of any state. "The other thing that I think is really important in addition to business leadership with a focus on athletics, is a broader appreciation and support for that top-twenty-five goal."

Then it was back to the money.

"I'd also like to have someone with tremendous, tremendous energy and fundraising ability," said Andy Haggard. "I know the Boosters are, of course, our fundraising arm here at Florida State, but nothing has to stop the athletic director from also being a fundraiser."

Mark Hillis worried that Florida State wouldn't be able to

afford an athletic director like the Domino's executive at Michigan. Ed Burr added that, to justify the high salary, the successful candidate would need to demonstrate an appreciation for the importance of television revenue in the modern-day college athletics program.

"The business of athletics," he said, "is the business of media and television these days."

The attitude expressed at the board meeting sums up the priorities of many universities when it comes to their athletic programs, something that might have had Duke's Dr. William Preston Few rolling over in his grave. Though the FSU meeting was in 2013, the mentality that drove the discussion took root over previous decades during the reign of Coach Bobby Bowden, as the crown jewel of Florida's state capital completed its transformation from a segregated college for white women into a modern public university and football powerhouse.

It was a transformation that sidelined academics. With the rise of the powerful Boosters, a driven fan base, and an administration fully committed to the importance of football in shaping their school's identity, some professors found themselves increasingly baffled and demoralized.

One of them was Ned Stuckey-French, who thought he knew more than most of his fellow English professors about football, having grown up in a big college sports town up north and played football in high school and at Harvard. Still, teaching at Florida State has been eye-opening—starting with the realization that incoming students must go to the football stadium at Champions Way to get acclimated.

"Right from the beginning, when you go there for orientation, immediately they let you know who's in charge," he said.

In one of the first basic English courses that he taught in the early 2000s, Stuckey-French had a football player who "was basically illiterate" and should not have been in college. The player, who eventually was drafted into the NFL, would "turn in writing assignments that were a handful of sentence fragments. I could tell he felt scared.

"They're just there to keep them eligible to play for a couple of years, with no real intention of an education," he said. "The NFL has this good thing going where the schools are essentially the farm league for the players."

Florida State University is far from alone in allowing itself to be a part of this system, of course. From coast to coast, institutions of higher learning, most of them public universities, have eagerly grabbed at the brass ring of big-time athletics, convinced it will unlock a magical doorway to riches and respect. And it is that out-of-control quest for money, and competition for status, that is at the root of academic scandals and criminal behavior that make headlines.

If not for the athletic scholarships granted to them, courtesy of millions in tax-exempt donations from boosters, many athletes who would never qualify academically for acceptance, wind up dominating attention and resources, and sometimes cause untold damage to a school's reputation and standards. How does that square with Florida State's mission statement, which doesn't even mention athletics, but talks bracingly about how the university "is dedicated to excellence in teaching, research, creative endeavors, and service"? More broadly, how did sports programs become the public face of so many universities and colleges?

Here's one way to begin to understand it: a few years ago the

BCS Coaches' Trophy, a $30,000 piece of Waterford crystal hand-crafted in the shape of a football, was accidentally knocked off its stand at the University of Alabama and shattered. What happened next could serve as a metaphor for the irrepressible allure of college sports: the Crimson Tide's athletic department swept up the jagged pieces and auctioned them off for $105,000.

Even broken beyond repair, the crystal football was worth more than what it cost to make it.

That, in fact, is the operating theory that animates big-time college athletics. University presidents and trustees come to believe that a strong sports program—football especially—will reap dividends far in excess of their investment. Embracing the argument of Coach Pee Wee Forsythe from a century earlier, modern-day higher-education officials insist that a successful sports program is the "front porch" that introduces an institution to the world, confers status, and stimulates gift-giving by wealthy alumni.

For a handful of teams at the very top of the NCAA Division I heap, that can be true. Only 20 of the 128 schools in the Football Bowl Subdivision—the crème de la crème of Division I—generate more money than they spend. Most FBS athletic programs are heavily funded by outside revenue, like ticket sales, booster donations, and television contracts. No doubt, for some of these schools, there is also the hard-to-measure benefit of national name recognition, as well as increased state resources and private donor interest.

But even allowing for that possibility, empirical evidence of it is difficult to find. A few months after one of the Seminoles' championship games, Tom Jennings, a top Florida State administrator, talked to a Seminoles news web site, Warchant.com, and seemed hard pressed to find an example of the wondrous side benefits that had flowed from it. He said an inspired athletics booster had come forward and offered $200,000 for new instruments for the marching band. Jennings, who ran the university's foundation, cautioned that winning seasons were not necessarily responsible for an uptick in donations.

"It's hard to link them specifically to those national championships," he said, "but I can tell you it didn't hurt."

Undergraduate applications also rose as the Seminoles advanced into the bowl season, another supposed perk cited by boosters. Yet, here too, school officials could not draw a connection between the two.

"There's nothing that stood out in my mind that we saw a tremendous surge," Janice Finney, Florida State's admissions director, told Warchant.com. "I think that's just a happenstance."

The reality is that the vast majority of schools that take the plunge into big-time college athletics not only fail to reap tangible benefits, but soon find themselves struggling to reach the top of an escalator that is headed downward with increasing speed. Too many high-level sports programs, tangential to the core mission of most schools, become sinkholes where precious resources and hard-won reputations for integrity vanish.

Outside the top tier of winningest schools, other athletic departments in the FBS lost an average of $17.6 million in 2013, as median total athletics expenses rose 10.6 percent. Trying to keep pace with rising costs, schools have increased mandatory athletic fees charged to all students and devoted an increasing portion of tuition revenue to sports. In the University of Virginia system, where student-athlete scholarships and coaches' salaries are the biggest drivers of athletic spending, some schools spend close to one-quarter of total tuition and fee revenue on sports. The increased spending is necessary because none of the 280 teams at Virginia's fifteen higher education institutions generate enough revenue to cover their expenses.

In fact, big-time sports programs are embraced by universities for reasons that don't always make much practical sense. State schools, in particular, can often draw upon a strong built-in fan base with a sense of regional pride. In these settings, a college sports program becomes entwined in a community's sense of identity. That emotional resonance can carry into state legislatures, often populated with alumni of the same public universities, who wield influence over decisions on taxpayer financing of such things as new stadiums and athletic facilities.

And woe to those who would try to alter the status quo.

After the University of Alabama at Birmingham decided to end its money-losing Division I football program in 2014 and plow the $10 million in annual savings into academics, its president was vilified and his job put at risk. Donors threatened to pull funding, and an angry mob punched the president's car and screamed obscenities as he left a meeting under police escort. Rather than acknowledge a courageous acceptance of hard fiscal realities, the head of the NCAA declared the university's decision "unfortunate."

The university's bold stand lasted about six months before it announced football was being reinstated. Boosters, business leaders, and politicians raised private money and pressed the board of trustees, injecting the issue into a search to replace some departing members. A state lawmaker from Birmingham who led the charge, Jack Williams, crowed that a university with a resurgent football program would be the "vehicle to get us to greatness.

"I knew if we kept the pressure on the board and administration that eventually folks would rally to our side," he said, "because we were standing up for a community that desperately needed success."

———

Chances are that Dr. William Preston Few would have approved of Florida State's choice of a new athletic director in the summer of 2013: Stan Wilcox, a Duke University man and the first African-American to hold the job at FSU.

Granted, Wilcox wasn't the CEO of Domino's Pizza, but he had a decent business-oriented resume. As the deputy athletic director at Duke, he had been in charge of football operations, and before that had been an assistant commissioner for the Big East Conference, where he was involved in negotiating television and marketing deals—something Florida State's board of trustees appreciated. In fact, Dr. Eric Barron, Florida State's president, reminded everyone during the announcement of Wilcox's hiring that bringing in more money would be a top priority.

"My sense is we need to be looking at every possible revenue stream and working to enhance opportunities and be able to turn that right back and invest in our programs," said Dr. Barron, praising Wilcox's "exceptional portfolio of strategic planning and fundraising experience and his reputation as a motivator, effective communicator, and facilitator."

And, lest anyone forget: ". . . as well as a commitment to the education of our student athletes."

UNCLE LUKE

Devonta Freeman really wanted to wear a No. 24 jersey while starting as a running back for the Florida State Seminoles in 2011.

Like Ernie Sims III a decade earlier, Freeman had his reasons for coveting a particular jersey number. Sims had wanted No. 34 because his brother, Michael Gibson, the serial rapist who was briefly with the Seminoles, had worn the same number. For Freeman, No. 24 had an altogether different meaning.

That's how old his beloved aunt, Tamekia Brown, was when she died of a heart attack in the violent Miami housing projects where she and Freeman grew up. Freeman, who had six younger brothers and sisters and had had to take on the role of man of the house at age twelve, was heartbroken when Tamekia died. He was fourteen at the time.

"She meant so much to me," Freeman said. "She was like the world to me. She was one of the younger aunties that I had, so we used to relate the most. We were real close. And she did my dreads before she passed away. She's just my favorite."

But he found that, at Florida State, jersey No. 24 was already spoken for. One of his teammates, Terrance Smith, wore it in honor of his father, who had played football at Clemson University. Freeman had to settle for No. 8 instead. But he didn't kick up a fuss. That wasn't Freeman's way.

If players like Jameis Winston seemed to believe the world revolved around them, Freeman had no such pretenses. He was the anti-Jameis. At Florida State, while Winston was getting into trouble with BB gun shootouts and a rape allegation, Freeman was using $300 of his financial aid to help Tamekia's children buy new clothes for school. He sent money back home for his mother and grandmother. The phone calls he got from Miami were not always eagerly awaited; once, after celebrating a big football victory, he was awakened in the middle of the night by his sobbing sister, with the news that a twenty-year-old cousin had been shot dead.

Freeman had grown up in the Liberty City section of Miami, a notorious neighborhood plagued by gangs and drugs, where the local funeral home was always busy with services for young black men killed for no good reason. Freeman was all too familiar with that ritual: one of the many odd jobs he juggled as a kid to help put food on the table was giving out flowers and greeting mourners arriving at the mortuary. At $50 per funeral—sometimes at a rate of four per day—he found it paid better than his other gigs at the gas station and doing yard work.

Like a lot of disadvantaged kids from inner city hellholes, Freeman didn't have a lot of support to help him academically in school. He gravitated to sports, where he excelled at football, despite his relatively small size—he is a muscular five feet, eight inches. What he lacked in heft, he more than made up for in speed, agility, and just plain grit. Freeman would pinball down the field, unafraid to get hit, sometimes running over tacklers when he couldn't elude them. And he also made an impression off the field, where his sunny demeanor belied the harshness of his surroundings. He quickly caught the attention of the co-founder of the Liberty City Optimist football club where he played: Luther Campbell, a.k.a. Uncle Luke.

"Devonta Freeman was one of the nicest, sweetest kids I've ever known," Campbell said. "He was well mannered, soft-spoken, just a lovable kid. He was also one of the most gifted athletes I've ever seen."

Uncle Luke, who had first noticed Freeman's athletic potential as a nine-year-old playing baseball, had also grown up in Liberty City and helped start the nonprofit football club as a way to try to keep vulnerable boys out of trouble. Over the years, Campbell's club produced numerous players who would be eagerly recruited by colleges and even go on to the pros. He attributed it to the seriousness with which they took the game.

"Their dedication and concentration was phenomenal, because they used the game to block out all the hell they experienced on the streets and at home," he said. "Most kids in youth sports, they're doing it for fun, or because their parents want them to do it, but for the kids from Liberty City and Overtown, football provided a dream and a mission and purpose in life."

Campbell took Freeman under his wing, encouraging his football career and becoming an invaluable dispenser of wisdom, so much so that Freeman has described him as "a second father to me." Giving Freeman a ride back home to the projects after games, Campbell would tell him he had to take charge in his house in order to help his mother, Lorraine, who struggled to raise the family alone while Freeman's father was in prison.

"He was like, 'Man, you're going to have to grow up and be the man of the house,'" said Freeman. "I was looking at my momma,

I watched her do things that I never want to see her do, just to bring food and pay bills. When he told me that, I told myself I wasn't ever going to ask my momma for nothing else again."

Campbell also impressed upon him the need to be a positive role model for his younger siblings.

"I was warning him that if he ever got caught up in dope-dealing and killing other young black men, the odds of his brothers and sisters following a similar dark path would increase," Campbell said.

As for whether Uncle Luke himself was a positive role model, well, that's another story.

There's a photo that captures perfectly the contradiction of Luther Campbell.

In it, Campbell is clad in a football jersey, facing the camera with his trademark gap-toothed grin, looking like the amiable coach and mentor that so many boys know him to be. Crouching before him, also facing the camera, is a platinum-haired woman, wearing six-inch heels and nothing else, her legs spread wide and shaved vagina presented to the world. The photo was part of a promotion for an adult entertainment business Campbell ran at the same time he was involved with youth football.

Uncle Luke—who is the former front man for the notorious 1980s rap group 2 Live Crew—in many ways is the inevitable result of the absence of a sanity code. For all his positive influences, there is a flip side that embodies the coarse, money-fueled culture enveloping so much of college sports. Campbell has been a shameless purveyor of raunchy music and videos, with an arrest record and a keen sense of self-promotion. His Instagram page has photos of college and high school football players mixed with shots of half-naked women and himself giving the finger to the camera. His social media accounts are sort of a stream of consciousness of plugs for his business activities, along with asides about sports, music, and whatever else is on his mind.

During his days with 2 Live Crew—whose explicit lyrics were banned in places and led to a Supreme Court free-speech ruling in Campbell's favor—the group's badass persona became intertwined with that of the University of Miami Hurricanes football team. On one of 2 Live Crew's album covers, members of the band wore team jackets. Campbell recorded a Hurricanes fight song, "The U," and became sort of a team mascot, throwing victory parties at South Beach nightclubs, when not cruising around the bay in his fifty-foot yacht, *Scandalous*, and being pursued for child support by some of the five women with whom he had kids.

In later years, in between performing, pitching his own brand of booze, and holding forth in the Miami media, Campbell was not only helping run the Liberty City Optimists, but also was serving as defensive coordinator for the football teams at Miami's Northwestern and Norland high schools. It was a peculiar role for him, and one that defied an attempt by state education officials to halt it.

The state of Florida tried to deny him a certification to coach, pointing to his criminal record and business history as evidence that he failed "to maintain good moral character." In a court filing, the state declared that he had "produced and published pornographic materials, promoting, among other things, the exploitation and denigration of women."

The state also detailed a string of criminal charges Campbell faced dating to 1979 when he was convicted of improper display of a firearm. Six years later, while riding in a vehicle, he was arrested and fined for possessing a semiautomatic handgun concealed inside a ski mask. That same year he was charged with inciting a riot, but the case was dismissed. In 1986, he was convicted of improper exhibition of a firearm. Over the next decade, he would be arrested six more times on charges ranging from aggravated assault with a weapon to battery, all of which were dismissed. Most of the cases stemmed from brawls in bars and nightclubs.

In 2003, he was arrested in South Carolina on charges of "aiding or procuring a person to expose body parts in a lewd and lascivious manner—namely, the insertion of a soda bottle by two strippers into the vagina of a member of the audience who climbed onstage during a performance, as well as several acts of unspecified obscenities by two male members of the audience with the aforesaid strippers. The charge was that these unlawful acts were in the presence of and with the encouragement of" Campbell. Campbell received a suspended sentence in exchange for an agreement not to perform in the state for five years.

Finally, Campbell was arrested in 2009 and charged with contempt of court for failing to pay $10,000 in a child support case. The disposition of that case was unclear, but Campbell was released, and claimed it involved a dispute over legal fees.

In the end, the state was overruled by an administrative law judge. The judge, in a lengthy opinion, acknowledged the state's central concern that Campbell might not be suitable to serve as a role model. What would kids make, he wondered, of Campbell's dual status as molder of young minds and purveyor of "entertainment efforts along the lines of 'Suck This Dick,' 'We Want Big Dick,' 'Hoes,' 'Pop That Pussy' and 'South Beach Bitches'?

"Impressionable inner-city youth might be easily confused by these competing messages, as they compared the paltry sums paid their contract coaches and modest sums paid their regular coaches and teachers, with the riches lavished upon the producers of adult entertainment," the judge wrote, before concluding that Campbell nevertheless should be allowed to coach.

The judge cited testimony from coaches and others who spoke movingly of Campbell's devotion to helping disadvantaged kids and his ability to connect with them, given his own rough-and-tumble upbringing in Liberty City. Campbell, the judge wrote, "got kids off the dangerous streets and onto the football field."

He "has decided to help the most vulnerable, most at-risk students from the inner-city neighborhood where he grew up," said the judge, adding that Campbell "has served these students in ways that other persons would find difficult, if not impossible, to replicate."

But the judge's thinking rested, at least in part, on the notion that Campbell's involvement in sexually explicit materials was limited to the crude lyrics associated with his time, in the distant past, as a singer for 2 Live Crew, and that he had since moved on to more respectable ventures. However, what state education officials seemed to have overlooked was that his more recent efforts to launch a business centered almost entirely around adult entertainment.

There were several iterations of it between 2002 and 2008, including a web site called Unclelukesworld, which featured links to various pornographic productions: "Explore Luke's XXX Files, Amazing XXX galleries, video clips, Freakshow movies, Live feeds and much more." Another site, xxxluke.com, featured adult movies Campbell was promoting, including one that was to be based around a party to be held in Miami in which he would supposedly take part. An announcement posted on the site, dated January 16, 2004, and titled "The Man Who Put the Sex into Rap Becomes a Sex Professional," boasted that "Campbell intends to go further sexually on camera than other hip-hop artist that has [sic] been involved in porn has. While he may do more than just hosting, the extent of his sexual involvement isn't set in stone yet—he could end up going all the way." It doesn't appear that he did.

A detailed, twenty-one-page business plan for Luke Enterprises set out a goal of producing adult content that included "softcore, hardcore and music" delivered through DVDs, web sites, magazines, and nightclubs, saying, "Luther Campbell is poised to construct the urban equivalent to the Playboy empire.

"The old adage 'sex sells' is magnified by the prospect of Luke Campbell acting as chief salesman."

There was also another relevant issue that the state did not dwell on in its case against Campbell: his murky activities at the intersection of money and college sports.

One of the people listed in the business plan as a member of "the team" that was supposed to run Campbell's sex-themed enterprise was Sean Allen, a co-founder of another of Campbell's one-time ventures called Luke Sports & Entertainment, which was envisioned as a talent management agency for athletes and music artists. But it never really went anywhere. After that effort sputtered, Allen and Campbell briefly explored starting another sports agency with Nevin Shapiro, a wealthy booster of the University of Miami Hurricanes football team with whom Allen had previously worked.

That proposal did not materialize, either—fortunately for Campbell. It turned out that Shapiro was a crook. He would later be convicted of running a $930 million Ponzi scheme and sent to prison for twenty years—prompting him to unleash a torrent of allegations about illicit gifts and cash he said he and Allen showered on University of Miami football players. Shapiro's lurid accusations included greasing players and recruits with prostitutes, Cadillacs, and visits to strip clubs, doling out tens of thousands in cash, and paying for a woman's abortion after a player got her pregnant.

Allen corroborated many of Shapiro's stories, and added a few of his own. One of them involved Devonta Freeman.

Being from Miami, Freeman had wanted to play for the Hurricanes. Luther Campbell—a big University of Miami fan—had tried to get the school interested in Freeman, without success. So he took Freeman on a visit upstate, where Florida State coach Jimbo Fisher took an immediate liking to the dynamic running back and successfully recruited him.

But at the eleventh hour, literally the day before Freeman was supposed to start classes at Florida State in 2011, the University of Miami tried to get Freeman to change his mind. A new coach, Al Golden, had just started there and one of his assistants had Sean Allen call Freeman to put the arm on him. Allen peppered Freeman with phone calls, at one point even getting his mother on a conference call with Coach Golden, to no avail.

Later, Allen expressed regrets about pressuring the young player and his family.

"I had never asked a player to change schools," he told the *Miami Herald*. "I immediately felt bad about putting Devonta in such an uncomfortable situation."

Allen didn't implicate Campbell in that episode, and said he didn't know much about dealings Campbell might have had with Shapiro. From his prison cell, however, Shapiro had a few things to say about Uncle Luke; in an interview with Yahoo Sports he viewed himself as carrying on a tradition that Campbell had started years before.

Shapiro was referring to Campbell's own brush with college football infamy back in 1994, when a *Miami Herald* investigation concluded that he and some NFL players had paid members of the University of Miami football team cash bounties for making big plays. The cash was reportedly delivered to the athletes at one of Campbell's nightclubs. Campbell denied it, and he was never charged with any NCAA violations.

But the following year, after he flew into a rage when Miami didn't include in its starting lineup a black quarterback he liked, Campbell suddenly threatened to spill the beans on violations at the university: "If they don't start Ryan Collins, the University of Miami will get the death penalty. I will tell all. I will tell everything I know to the NCAA."

It doesn't appear that he did. Whatever the case, an impression was left of Campbell as a rogue college football booster, prowling the sidelines and mixing with players off the field in ways that sometimes tested the boundaries of propriety. Years later, Nevin Shapiro fancied himself a modern-day version of Uncle Luke.

"Luther Campbell was the first uncle who took care of players before I got going," Shapiro said. "His role was diminished by the NCAA and the school and someone needed to pick up that mantle. That someone was me. He was Uncle Luke and I became Little Luke."

Campbell took issue with the comparison and sued him for libel.

"That punk could never be me," said Campbell, who later dropped the suit. "It has never been about money for me. It has always been about community service. That's what being Uncle Luke is really about."

As usual with Luther Campbell, though, reality was more complicated. A clearer picture of what Uncle Luke was really about would come into focus on the glorious day when Florida State's Devonta Freeman finally achieved personal "bigness and prosperity" and signed a multimillion-dollar contract to play in the National Football League.

MORAL COMPASS

When Christie Suggs sat down to fill out her Free Application for Federal Student Aid for the 2013–14 school year, the numbers were ugly.

By then, she had been a doctoral student at Florida State for four years. Christie had paid for most of that with federal loans, and still had debt left from her bachelor's and master's degrees. All told, she had $141,032 in loans outstanding, most of which were unsubsidized, meaning they had higher interest rates. But it was worse than that.

Her income for the prior year, as a teaching assistant and instructor of online classes, was only $36,486; she got an education tax credit of $280. Christie was raising her son, now eleven, by herself without regular child support from her estranged husband. And she was ineligible for federal education grants for low-income students because she was no longer an undergrad. What's more, her FAFSA student aid report noted that she had previously declared bankruptcy, and warned that she had already borrowed more money than allowed under federal student loan limits.

Still, Christie was nothing if not an optimist. She dreamed of using her online teaching skills to work from home in some tropical locale. While taking classes and commuting from Alabama, she kept angling to find an apartment that would be closer to the university and allow her son, Hunter, to start going to a decent public school.

In the summer of 2013, she had just finished her first semester as a teaching assistant at the Dedman School of Hospitality and happily shared the news with coworkers that she had signed a lease for an apartment in Tallahassee. She was hopeful about getting more money in the fall. Under the workload rubric followed by Dedman, teaching assistants for online courses were expected to be responsible for one hundred students for every ten hours they worked. Christie let her supervisor know she wanted to work as many hours as possible, and was told she might be able to get thirty hours a week—or three hundred students.

Others might have found that daunting, but friends said Christie welcomed the challenge. Barbara Davis, another older student in the PhD program at Florida State, became close to Christie, and the two would share many evenings helping each other with school projects, playing Scrabble, and sleeping over at each other's apartments. Christie was a gifted teacher, Davis said.

"It was marvelous to watch her prepare and position herself for the start of an online synchronous lecture. She had an inviting lilt in her voice as she greeted every student as they logged in," said Davis. "She expressed alternating patience and exuberance as she worked through the lecture, pausing effortlessly for questions and always ending on time."

Christie's work ethic and cheerful demeanor were appreciated by students and coworkers, too. In earlier courses she taught outside of Dedman, students liked her patient but firm guiding hand that held them accountable while also giving them a fair chance to succeed. It showed in their evaluations of her:

"Professor Suggs is amazing! She is very supportive in her teaching and encourages all students to learn."

"The instructor was wonderful!! Her comments were thought-provoking and meaningful. She was able to help right away whenever I had any questions and went above and beyond."

"She was a great teacher. She knows how to convey the lessons in a way that you can understand and the information stays with you. One can tell that she really enjoys her job and does it well."

Once at Dedman, Christie also did well. Her supervisor let her know that Dr. Mark Bonn, the head of distance learning at Dedman, liked her efforts to incorporate the concept of environmental sustainability into the Coffee & Tea course he taught and asked that her work be circulated as an example for other TAs. She started out enjoying her time there.

But as summer was drawing to a close, Christie had seen another side to higher education that she wasn't prepared for. Before Dedman, she had taught students who were serious about learning and starting a career. She helped with advanced courses in education at Florida State and psychology at Kaplan University. But at the hospitality school, athletes signed up for classes about wine and coffee because they were easy, and many of them weren't there to really learn anything; they simply needed to maintain a minimum grade point average to stay eligible to play their sport.

And yet, even in this accommodating environment, some athletes weren't able to keep up. Christie encountered problems with at least six Seminoles football players who missed deadlines, skipped assignments, or handed in plagiarized work. To be sure, other students did as well. But as she attempted to hold the athletes to the same academic standards as everybody else, she found herself undermined and stymied. They got breaks that other students didn't.

The Seminoles' star running back, James Wilder Jr., was a case in point.

Like his father, James Wilder Jr. was a natural athlete. The elder Wilder had played professional football for ten years, mostly with the Tampa Bay Buccaneers. Father and son were both running backs, each over six feet tall and lanky, though James Jr. was a little more muscular than his dad and could twist and pivot to elude tacklers like a gymnast.

The younger Wilder was widely considered the top recruit in the country, an All-American, when Florida State nabbed him in 2010 from Henry B. Plant High School in Tampa, where he rushed for 1,600 yards and twenty-two touchdowns in his final season. ESPN gushed: "There might not be a more freakish athlete and more impressive prospect from a size to speed standpoint than Wilder II. The NFL lineage is definitely apparent when watching him shred opposing defenses as a running back."

As Wilder described it at the time, Florida State's coaches had achingly pursued him. "They said, 'We know we can sleep well as long as we're in your top three. But we can sleep great when we know you're going to be a Seminole.' So I called Coach [Fisher] two days ago and said, 'Coach, I know you slept well last night, but tonight you'll be able to sleep great.' He just yelled and he passed the phone to all the coaches and they were yelling."

When Wilder got to Florida State, he didn't disappoint. In his first two years, after a slow start his freshman season, he ran for nearly eight hundred yards and scored twelve touchdowns. Off the field, however, his immaturity was showing.

On the morning of February 22, 2012, Leon County sheriff's deputy Donald Bramblett knocked on an apartment door near the Florida State campus looking for Bianca Camarda, a young woman with an outstanding arrest warrant for failure to appear in court on a criminal mischief charge. The nineteen-year-old Wilder answered the door and told the deputy that Camarda wasn't there. Bramblett asked if he could come in and look around, and Wilder agreed. In the apartment, Bramblett found Camarda hiding in the bathroom. He placed her in handcuffs.

"After we exited the bathroom," the deputy wrote in his report, "Mr. Wilder stepped between me and Ms. Camarda and told me, 'She's not going to jail.' I then reached around Wilder to regain control of Camarda. Wilder then pushed my arm away and again told me that 'she's not going.'"

Wilder, according to Bramblett, continued blocking him until the deputy unholstered his Taser and led Camarda outside to his cruiser. But Wilder ran up behind him, "yelling obscenities" and insisting that Bramblett was not going to leave with his girlfriend. When a sergeant arrived and asked Wilder for some identification, according to the report, Wilder responded, "I don't have to give you a fucking thing."

The officers decided they'd had enough and placed Wilder under arrest. Initially, the charges against him were battery of an officer and resisting arrest with violence. A few hours later, however, the latter charge was downgraded from a felony count to resisting *without* violence, a first-degree misdemeanor. Still, because the battery charge was a felony, school policy dictated that he be suspended from the team pending the outcome of his case. Not that it mattered much, since it was the off-season and football practice wouldn't start for another month.

Representing Wilder was the go-to criminal defense attorney for Florida State athletes in trouble, R. Timothy Jansen. He told the press that Wilder's actions had been misunderstood, and that he had simply been trying to show Deputy Bramblett text messages from his girlfriend's public defender indicating she didn't need to be arrested.

"Hopefully we can resolve this," Jansen said. "We certainly don't want his career to end because of this."

In the coming months, however, Wilder didn't help his cause. Jansen had worked his magic, getting the crucial felony count of battery dropped and having Wilder plead no contest to the misdemeanor charge, allowing him to rejoin the football team. Under his plea deal, Wilder was on probation for six months and was supposed to spend nine days in a county work camp, attend an anger management class, and pay $165 in court costs. But he did none of those things.

That June, he was arrested again for violating the terms of his probation after he tested positive for alcohol, and jailed. Jansen was back on the case.

"We're going to try and see if we can get it resolved," he said. "We hope to get him in court next week."

Jansen got Wilder out and smoothed things over with the court. But Wilder still couldn't stay out of trouble. In January 2013, he was arrested yet again, this time for missing a court date to answer to a charge of driving with a suspended license. The string of run-ins with the law, all of which drew negative attention in the media, was threatening to derail his prospects. Wilder's father tried to buck him up, saying, "Just keep moving forward."

"He likes to take life situations and give them a football aspect," Wilder said of his dad. " 'That was first down. You've got to focus on second down. You lost two yards on the first down, you've got to focus on the second down.' "

Jansen again helped Wilder get through it and back onto the field. The running back was just one of several clients from Florida State who were keeping Jansen busy as the 2013 football season was getting under way. Another, of course, was Jameis Winston, the quarterback whose rape accusation, so far, had been kept quiet by athletic officials and the police.

A lesser-known Florida State client of Jansen's, however, wasn't on the football team, although he was no stranger to it. He was Dr. Mark Bonn—Christie Suggs's boss at the Dedman School of Hospitality.

While Jansen was helping James Wilder Jr. navigate the court system for the third time in 2013, he was also tending to the legal problems of Dr. Bonn, whose second wife had filed for divorce and obtained a restraining order against him. (The order was eventually lifted with no admission of wrongdoing by Dr. Bonn.) Jansen, a criminal defense lawyer whose practice areas include domestic violence, represented him in the civil proceeding.

It was the second time Dr. Bonn had been accused of domestic abuse. In 1998, when he was divorced from his first wife, he was charged with domestic battery; he pleaded not guilty and the case was later dropped.

That earlier case also occurred while he was working at Florida State, where he had been since 1989, when he joined the college of business as an associate professor. By 1998, he been named director of graduate studies in hospitality and tourism at Dedman, and in 2009 he added director of distance learning to his portfolio. He created Dedman's online "beverage management" courses dealing with wine, beer, and coffee.

Dr. Bonn always had an affinity for sports. He had been co-captain of the baseball team at Furman University, a small liberal arts school in South Carolina; forty years later, he still proudly listed his .338 batting average on his LinkedIn page. While attending Appalachian State University as a graduate student in resort management, he also coached the baseball team.

At Florida State, he forged a close relationship with Seminoles athletics, which had natural tie-ins with Dedman through courses in golf and recreation management. In fact, the hospitality school was a frequent recipient of donations from boosters, among them the niece of Ron Sellers—the former Florida State football star who had graciously ceded his claim to jersey No. 34 so Coach Bobby Bowden could recruit Ernie Sims III—who pledged $1.7 million to Dedman.

Dr. Bonn himself got in on the fundraising. He partnered with a booster group called Old School, which held joint fundraisers, some featuring Bowden, benefiting a charity run by Coach Jimbo Fisher as well as the Dedman school. At one of them, Dr. Bonn accepted a ceremonial $20,000 check to help support the wine program at Dedman.

Student athletes couldn't take Dr. Bonn's wine and beer classes until they were twenty-one years old. But a lot of them signed up for Coffee & Tea, including James Wilder, Jr.

On Thursday, July 25, 2013, Wilder sent an email to Dr. Bonn worrying about his grade in the course, saying he had missed an assignment and three quizzes, and pasting some overdue work at the bottom of the message. He said he expected to get a B and needed to "keep myself in good academic place with the school."

Within an hour, Dr. Bonn, who was traveling in St. Louis, forwarded the email to Christie and responded himself to Wilder, asking that he come to his office the following Monday or Tuesday. Dr. Bonn asked Christie what Wilder's grade was in the course. She replied that he was failing, partly because of his missed work and because his final project did not include two sections.

"His average is now a 57.2%," she replied. "At this point even if we accept this late work he emailed to you, and he gets 100% on the remaining work, he will still only get a D in the course."

What followed was a flurry of emails over the next few days in which Dr. Bonn appeared to search for ways to allow Wilder to make up missed assignments and add the missing sections to his final project—which had already been graded by Christie. Dr. Bonn instructed Christie to give Wilder till 5 p.m. Saturday to hand in his missing project sections. That deadline came and went with nothing from Wilder.

Christie shared her concerns about giving Wilder a special break with Aiden Sizemore, the program associate at Dedman who had complained in an email to her about Dr. Bonn's "favoritism for athletes." Sizemore called Dr. Bonn's requests on behalf of Wilder "unorthodox" and said he'd take it up with the head of the hospitality school. But nothing came of that.

Meanwhile, over the weekend, Dr. Bonn was still making allowances for Wilder, to whom he referred in an email to Christie as a "star running back." He told Christie to contact Wilder and extend his deadline again.

"Send him an email asking him to confirm receipt and confirm he will agree to submitting the work," Dr. Bonn wrote. "Give him 24 hours from the time he replies to your email and please copy me on everything."

By Monday, Wilder still had not handed in his late work and was supposed to meet with Dr. Bonn that day. But at three thirty on Monday morning, he sent Dr. Bonn a one-line message saying he couldn't make it. "Sir the Tuesday conference world [*sic*] actually be better for me sir I wanna if it's ok switch till Tuesday."

Dr. Bonn was accommodating. "Ok James. What time? 10? Can you please call me?"

Four hours later, still nothing.

"James," Dr. Bonn plaintively wrote, "can you see me at 12 noon tomorrow in my office please? Please confirm. I have meetings before and following this, so I do need you to confirm. Thank you."

Finally, on Thursday, August 1, Wilder emailed his missing project sections to Dr. Bonn, saying he had also completed his missed quizzes. He added, "My grade in the class should be a B now."

"Thanks for working with me as I truly appreciate it," Wilder said.

Dr. Bonn forwarded Wilder's missing work to Christie.

"It looks great," he said.

Deciding to share her concerns about Dr. Bonn and the favored treatment of athletes with higher-ups at the university was a difficult move for Christie. Though hardly a shrinking violet—while living alone, she got in the habit of sleeping with a handgun under her pillow—Christie was also not the sort to go begging for a fight. She had always tried to see the best side of people.

The inspector general's office at Florida State is not primarily focused on academic issues. Rather, its emphasis is financial waste and fraud. Staff there spend most of their time conducting audits and doing background checks on new employees.

The chief auditor, Sam McCall, arranged a meeting with Christie and asked her to provide any documentation to back up her allegations. She forwarded email chains to McCall that detailed her dealings with Dr. Bonn and at least six starting members of the football team, and on August 26 she met with McCall and one of his investigators, Jeffrey Caines. A few days later, Christie was contacted by Carolyn Egan, the chief legal counsel for Florida State. Egan introduced herself as the university's attorney and asked that Christie consult with her right away.

"Please let me know when you are available tomorrow morning for a few additional questions that have arisen," Egan said. "We are trying to get to the bottom of the complex and important matters involved here and time is of the essence."

By then, Florida State should have been well aware of the institutional risk of mixing athletes and online courses, having weathered the *"Apollo 13"* scandal several years earlier that centered around that very issue. What is more, the administration was already cognizant of serious problems with Dr. Bonn's online beverage courses even before Christie went to the inspector general.

Unbeknownst to Christie, university officials had been privately voicing concerns about the integrity of the classes for at least a year. As one administrator put it in an email to a colleague, the issues involved "more than just the academic dishonesty," but also "student/faculty ratios in the DSH online classes and who are actually teaching the classes." The dean of the College of Business, Caryn Beck-Dudley, had pressed the director of Dedman to make changes, but little seemed to have been accomplished, prompting her to pull the plug on the courses for fall 2013.

"Clearly our discussion didn't make any difference in the outcome," Beck-Dudley told another administrator in early August 2013. "Maybe canceling the classes will have a greater impact."

After telling her story to university officials, more than a month went by and Christie had heard nothing more from the investigators or the university's lawyer.

Meanwhile, the Seminoles' football season started with a 41–13 thumping of Pittsburgh. Quarterback Jameis Winston led the team to one of its most decisive victories, and followed it up a week later with a 62–7 rout of Nevada—with running back James

Wilder Jr. scoring a touchdown. Then there was a 54–6 crushing of Bethune-Cookman. Next was a 48–34 win over Boston College and an astounding 63–0 shutout of Maryland.

It was an unprecedented run of success. Though the team's schedule was viewed as relatively easy, the size of the victories and Winston's performance grabbed headlines, boosting the Seminoles' stock in college football surveys. Florida State was being talked about as a possibly unstoppable force with the potential to go all the way to the football championship.

Increasingly nervous about the lack of feedback from the university administration, Christie reached out to Sam McCall in early October and was surprised to learn that the inspector general's office was no longer involved; the whole matter had been turned over to the attorney, Carolyn Egan. Christie waited, and increasingly fretted about losing her teaching assistant's job.

"I'm a little worried about my employment and just want to make sure I know what is going on with me so that if I am going to lose my job I go ahead now and start looking," Christie wrote to Dr. Jane Ohlin, the director of the Dedman school. "I am the sole support for my son and can't go any period without employment."

Officials within Dedman were now treading carefully with Christie. Dr. Ohlin authorized a pay raise of one dollar an hour for her and offered reassurance.

"You won't be losing your job here," Dr. Ohlin replied. "You have done a wonderful job for us, and you will be allowed to stay with us."

Still, the whole ordeal weighed heavily on Christie. She confided in friends and family details of what she was going through. Some of them wondered why she had bothered going out on a limb, given her precarious personal circumstances.

"They were asking her to pad grades for the football players, and I told her I thought that was common practice," said Phil Suggs, Christie's estranged husband. "But she said, 'Not with me. If they don't make it, they don't make it.'

"She was kind of naive that way," he said. "Christie was the smartest person I ever met, and she was a very nice person. But not always realistic."

Barbara Davis, Christie's friend and fellow student, said the grading controversy "was a huge heartache for her.

"She told me how there had been tremendous pressure on her to pass these football players, even though they didn't deserve it," Davis said.

Davis recalled another thing Christie told her: that as the 2013 football season progressed, Christie believed some people at Florida State were concerned that her accusations about the football players could jeopardize the Seminoles' chances at a championship. Athletes not in good academic standing cannot play in their sport, and the football team was in the midst of what would become only its third undefeated season in school history.

"I remember it was bowl time coming up," said Davis, "and they were worried about losing the players if they had failed Christie's course."

Christie's close friend Melissa Isaak, a lawyer in Alabama, also recalled Christie relating a similar story.

"She was told that what she did could lead to the shutdown of the football program at FSU," Isaak said. "But Christie had a pretty strong moral compass and just wasn't going to compromise on something like that."

BIG TIME

SCANDAL

Athletic departments have proven uniquely insensitive to sex crimes, which occur with such disturbing regularity that there are web sites devoted solely to tracking sexual assault cases in college sports.

Of course, colleges in general have struggled to deal with the problem of sexual assaults, not just in the sports realm. Title IX of federal education law requires schools to provide equal treatment to women, including safeguarding their right to be free from sexual harassment and abuse. Responding to public pressure, the federal government has pushed schools to get more aggressive in policing sexual improprieties. In 2011, the U.S. Department of Education sent a "Dear Colleague" letter to colleges, reminding them to put systems in place to address complaints by victims in a fair and supportive manner, and in 2013, Congress added more requirements when it reauthorized the Violence Against Women Act.

But many schools still fail to do enough to help female students, especially where athletes are concerned.

One would think that Baylor University of all places, which wears its Baptist Christian affiliation on its sleeve—its motto is

"For Church, For Texas"—would have zero tolerance for egregiously sinful behavior. The oldest continuously operating university in Texas, Baylor long had a middling reputation when it came to athletics, content to focus on its actual mission of educating students. But in recent decades it was drawn, like so many other schools, to the flame of big-time sports.

Baylor's budget for athletics skyrocketed more than 300 percent in the 2000s. It built a $266 million stadium and threw money at a hard-driving new coach, Art Briles, who took the football team from among the worst in the division to being a bowl contender. After seven years as head coach, Briles was being paid more than $4 million a year and Baylor's athletics revenues had topped $100 million for the first time—incredible for a small school that a decade earlier barely had eight thousand season-ticket holders.

The rapid success was built on terrible compromises. As an outside investigation later revealed, Baylor's athletic department had cut corners in recruiting players, failing to regularly follow procedures for "criminal background checks, request for records of any prior college disciplinary actions, and character reference screening forms." Two players the college had recruited had previously been dismissed from other schools for allegedly abusing young women, and once at Baylor, both were accused of sexual assault.

One of them, Sam Ukwuachu, was accused of raping a freshman soccer player, but the university cleared him after a cursory "investigation" of the case. That might have been the end of it had the victim not pursued justice elsewhere. Prosecutors charged Ukwuachu with sexual assault, and he was convicted and sentenced to six months in jail. The other, Shawn Oakman, was arrested on charges of raping a student at his apartment; he claimed the sex was consensual. Elsewhere on the football team,

Tevin Elliot was accused of sexual assault by five women over a three-year period, yet somehow he kept playing. He was eventually charged in one of the cases, convicted, and sentenced to twenty years in prison.

Finally, after the university's hand was forced by the cascading criminal cases and investigative reporting by ESPN, Coach Briles was fired and the athletic director resigned. The university's president—Kenneth Starr, the former independent counsel who had doggedly pursued accusations of sexual impropriety against Bill Clinton—stepped down but was allowed to remain for a time as chancellor.

A report by an outside law firm hired by the university's board found "significant concerns about the tone and culture within Baylor's football program as it relates to accountability for all forms of athlete misconduct." It also condemned the university administration as a whole for failing to properly investigate rape cases, and in the process, denying meaningful help and support to young women who had been violated.

"The investigations were conducted in the context of a broader culture and belief by many administrators that sexual violence 'doesn't happen here,'" the report said. "Administrators engaged in conduct that could be perceived as victim-blaming, focusing on the complainant's choices and actions, rather than robustly investigating the allegations, including the actions of the respondent."

As the report made clear, the many ways in which the school did not live up to its legal and moral obligations was breathtaking.

"Baylor failed to provide training and education to students; failed to identify and train responsible employees under Title IX; failed to provide clear information about reporting options and resources on campus; failed to have a centralized process for ensuring that all reports reached the Title IX coordinator; failed to impose appropriate interim measures in many cases; failed to appropriately evaluate and balance institutional safety and Title IX obligations against a complainant's request for anonymity or that no action/investigation be pursued against; failed to conduct prompt, equitable, adequate, and reliable investigations; failed to give complainants access to full range of procedural options under the policy; and failed to take sufficient action to identify, eliminate, prevent and address a potential hostile environment in individual cases.

"Institutional failures at every level of Baylor's administration directly impacted the response to individual cases and the Baylor community as a whole."

Unconscionable as it is, the poor response of schools to sexual assaults is arguably symptomatic of an even larger problem: an institutional aversion to scandal. Few things terrify college administrators more than the prospect of disgrace and reputational damage for any reason, be it sex assaults, academic cheating, gambling and other crimes, or violations arising from college athletic programs. It's not the acts themselves that make them fearful so much as the threat of public scrutiny and condemnation that follow.

Research for this book found that there have been at least 125 such scandals among the 345 NCAA Division I schools since the 1980s. The vast majority—some 102 of them—are concentrated among the 100 richest athletic programs. It would seem that administrators who are the most determined to maintain a big-time college sports program are often rewarded with the one thing they try hardest to avoid: a scandal.

With the increase in damaging off-field behavior comes the

impetus to cover up, soft-pedal, and deny. Universities are sometimes aided in that process by the authorities, who are compromised in their own way through economic forces as well as pride
in their local team and fear of the power behind it. The temptation to forsake institutional and community values in service of
the sport is arguably the most insidious byproduct of the academy's foray into big-time athletics.

The pressure to cut corners when problems develop, to look
the other way, comes from all directions. In what has been called
the "golden triangle" of intercollegiate athletics, media, and business, money drives everything, warping the decision-making of
all involved. With millions of dollars at stake, much of it riding
on undisciplined and undereducated young men from difficult
backgrounds, incremental bad choices get made that collectively
undermine faith in a community's institutions.

Can anyone recall police covering up an off-campus car crash
in the middle of the night because it involved a promising biology student? What about a dean of humanities personally recruiting a high school grad by giving a job to one of his relatives? Of
course not. But these things, and more, have occurred when the
beneficiary is an athlete.

When Arkansas state trooper Royce Denney pulled over two
cars traveling at nearly a hundred miles an hour, he was dismayed
to learn the driver of one of them was an Arkansas State University football player, Michael Dyer. His anxiety grew when he
allegedly found a gun and marijuana during the traffic stop and
became unsure how to handle the matter, given Dyer's involvement. An audio recording from Denney's cruiser caught him
telling Dyer that instead of arresting him, he'd take it up with
"Coach" and maybe give Dyer the gun back later.

"I really don't want to tell him about this because of the NCAA crap," Denney said. "I know there's a lot of stuff that goes on behind closed doors between coaches and players. I'm still in a predicament, even if I talk to Coach."

Denney was fired and Dyer was dismissed from the team after the incident came to light.

Like Baylor, Arkansas State is a top-100 athletic program financially, but doesn't compare to big-time schools like the University of Oklahoma, the third-largest employer in the city of Norman, with an athletic program that brings in $134 million a year. At Oklahoma, where football players have been involved in shootings, rape accusations, and selling cocaine to undercover cops, local law enforcement used to work with coach Barry Switzer to cover up minor crimes like public intoxication when they could: "The sheriff was a friend of the program," Switzer told *USA Today*. "He didn't want the publicity."

At the University of Nebraska—home to another of the highest-grossing sports programs, at more than $100 million— football coach Tom Osborne presided over a collection of violent criminals, including Christian Peter, who continued to play despite multiple arrests and sexual-assault accusations, and Lawrence Phillips, who took part in a championship game after being charged with throwing his girlfriend down a flight of stairs. But the Huskers under Osborne racked up wins, so Nebraskans cheered and, later, even voted the old coach into Congress.

Florida State University, too, has long endured suspicions that it is more concerned with damage control than doing the right thing when it comes to problematic athletes it recruits—and the suspicions go all the way to the top.

Almost from the moment when T. K. Wetherell assumed the presidency of Florida State in January 2003, he showed an unusual willingness to insert himself into sports controversies. A lawyer involved in a criminal case against a football player around that time was surprised to get a phone call from Wetherell, who was feeling around to see how bad the situation was for the university.

"T.K. said, 'Are you going to hurt us?'" recalled the lawyer, who did not want to be identified.

In another instance, after a Seminoles football player, Travis Johnson, was accused of sexual assault, Wetherell took the unprecedented step of personally speaking to both Johnson and his accuser, who was encouraged by the university to drop criminal charges. Florida State's vice president of student affairs sent an email to Johnson's accuser, asking her to consider a proposed settlement that Johnson had agreed to, which would "avoid embarrassment to himself, his family, the university and you." Under the proposal, Johnson would admit no wrongdoing, but would seek counseling and leave school for a semester, returning in time for football season.

The accuser, herself a student athlete, declined to accept the offer. Johnson's case went to trial and he was acquitted by an all-female jury, which was not swayed by the accuser's claim that, while she and Johnson had previously had a sexual relationship, they were no longer intimate when he forced himself on her one night. Meanwhile, an investigation by Florida State's inspector general found that the university had not followed proper protocol when its athletic department failed to refer the young woman's complaint to the police. The inspector general's report said the accuser, who at first preferred to have her complaint handled internally, only went to the police because she believed the school "was trying to cover up her allegations." Despite these findings, Wetherell continued to insist that school policies had been followed.

The prosecutor, Adam Ruiz, criticized the behavior of university officials as "bizarre, at best."

"There was an attempt to try and broker an agreement between her and the defendant so this case either would not go public or would not be sent to law enforcement," said Ruiz, adding, "That kind of behavior, that kind of thing, simply cannot be tolerated."

Ruiz said that in addition to Wetherell making his calls to Johnson and his accuser, Coach Bobby Bowden had tried to dissuade him from pressing ahead with the case. The experience was a wake-up call for Ruiz, a Florida transplant from up north who later left the prosecutor's office to go into private practice.

"I learned quickly what football meant in the South," recalled Ruiz. "Clearly, it meant a lot. And with respect to this case I learned that keeping players on the field was a priority."

If the Travis Johnson case in 2003 showed the difficulty of prosecuting allegations of sexual assault in a college town, the case of Greg Dent ten years later would become a painful reminder of that reality. It also served to illustrate the combustible nature of alcohol-fueled encounters between college students, as well as the complexities that confront authorities who try to unravel the facts of what happened and pursue justice.

Sheriff's deputy Georgia Northway was on duty late one night in June 2013 in a neighborhood not far from Florida State's campus when she was approached by a young woman on the street. The woman seemed upset and asked if she could get a ride home.

"I asked what was wrong, she said she just needed a ride home," Northway said, adding, "Her demeanor and body movement was very on edge, she appeared like she may have been crying. Looked a little disheveled."

The woman, D.R., wanted to know if she could use Northway's phone to call her father, who was also a deputy in another part of the state. Northway said she couldn't do that, but she did give D.R. a lift home. A few hours later, D.R. would call Tallahassee police and report that she had been sexually assaulted earlier that night by an old friend—Dent, a wide receiver on the Florida State football team.

D.R., who was twenty-one, and Dent, who was two years older, had known each other since the ninth grade and had never had a sexual relationship. She thought of him as a brother. They would hang out together, usually with other friends, and she would sometimes cook him dinner at her apartment.

On that night in June, after returning to Dent's apartment from an evening out drinking at a club with friends, D.R. decided to stay over, but there were only two choices of where to sleep: on the couch in the living room, where a friend of Dent's whom she didn't know was sleeping on an inflatable mattress, or in Dent's small bedroom. They ended up sharing Dent's bed, their heads at opposite ends because, she said, there was no intention of doing anything sexual.

D.R. said she awoke later to find Dent kissing and rubbing her. She told him "no," but Dent persisted.

"After a couple of increasingly forceful attempts to kiss and touch the victim, she bit Dent on his top lip," according to a police report. "Dent jumped out of the bed and the victim thought Dent had finally gotten the message."

He hadn't. He returned to bed and started pulling off D.R.'s shorts and underwear as she yelled at him to stop. As he tried to pull her legs apart—and, she said, partially penetrated her—she fought back, pulling his dreadlocks and hitting him until he jerked her with a little too much force and she tumbled to the floor. She jumped up, grabbed her clothes and left the apartment, hurriedly dressing herself outside the front door before leaving and encountering Deputy Northway.

Tallahassee police investigator Laura Gereg went to Dent's apartment and convinced him to come to the police department for an interview. After being read his Miranda rights, Dent proceeded to admit almost everything his accuser said, denying only that he ever penetrated her—though he "admitted to continuously attempting to penetrate the victim," according to Gereg, who said Dent even acknowledged that D.R. scratched him on the neck while telling him to stop and that he believed "she was probably drunk.

"She was, like, saying stop. She just kept saying stop," Dent said. "I just kept trying, kept trying. I was just trying to get on top of her. She was just saying stop, stop, stop . . ."

"Did you pull her legs apart at any point?" Gereg asked.

"I tried to."

Gereg seemed surprised at Dent's matter-of-fact admissions.

"Can you tell me a little bit about why, if she's consistently telling you to stop, why you kept trying to have sex with her?" she asked.

"I think it's probably 'cause I was a little too drunk," Dent replied, adding, "Pretty much 'cause she was in the room."

"So," Gereg said, "because you had a female there and you were drunk and you wanted to have sex, she was going to have to give it up."

"Yeah, pretty much."

Dent was charged with sexual assault—but his remarkable interrogation didn't see the light of day at the time. It was withheld from the press when Dent was arrested, under an exception to state public information laws for police records of admissions of guilt. Still, things looked precarious for Dent, as his attorney, the ubiquitous Tim Jansen, observed.

"It's a very serious offense, it's an offense that could send him to prison, if convicted," Jansen said. "It's certainly an offense that's going to get him suspended."

Dent's arrest came at a bad time for the Florida State football team, which was quickly losing players to injuries and other problems as they prepared for the start of the 2013 season. Receiver Willie Haulstead was out because of academic problems. Running back James Wilder Jr. was dealing with his own legal issues. The university had to suspend Dent because of the felony charge. As his case wended its way through the court system—during which Dent was jailed a second time for missing a court date—he eventually dropped out of Florida State altogether.

By the time Dent's case finally came to trial, circumstances had taken a turn in his favor. To the frustration of prosecutors, D.R. proved to be a difficult victim. Her conflicting emotions about Dent led her to contact him when she wasn't supposed to, and then not tell the prosecutors. Once she was on the witness stand, the jury was presented with a text message she sent to Dent at some point after the alleged assault:

> I think about you every day. Lord knows I miss you. You're my closest friend. I love you Greg. I want to make sure you know that.

"That's the first text message you send to your rapist," said Dent's attorney, Nathan Prince, noting that D.R. also made him cupcakes.

"That's the first text message I send to someone who was a friend and made a really, very poor decision," she responded. "I'm not thinking, 'Oh my God, this is my rapist.' I'm thinking this is someone I've known for years and years and years, and they messed up. He messed up really bad."

Rocking back and forth in the witness chair in obvious anxiety, D.R. explained her reticence about pressing charges and said it was only after she talked to her father that "I knew what happened wasn't right." But she feared ruining Dent's football career, saying, "I don't want to see him go to jail.

"I knew if I said something it would basically kind of end his life," she said. "Because of who he was on the team, it would spread quickly, people would find out. He would be attacked, I would be attacked. I didn't want that for him or myself."

For his part, Dent took the stand and insisted he thought he had "the go sign" from D.R. to have sex with her, despite her saying no. He said she acted flirtatious that evening by sticking close to him at the club, and that sharing his bed and getting into her night clothes were signals for him to proceed.

"Any more go signs?" asked the prosecutor, Stephanie Morris.

"Umm, she was allowing me to touch her," Dent said.

"But she told you no."

"Yeah, but also she never got up and left," he replied, adding, "She could've slept on my couch, but did she? No. She wanted to, she wanted to lay with me. So, automatically you can take that as a go sign, 'cause she never did it, she took her clothes off, I took my clothes off, she never said nothing about it, so I never thought nothing about it."

The entire trial lasted one day, and the jury came back with a verdict that evening: not guilty of sexual assault, but guilty of the lesser offense of misdemeanor battery. The jurors seemed to be trying to split the difference, acknowledging D.R.'s complaint that her old friend had crossed the line, while also giving a nod to Dent's insistence that she was a willing participant. Still, it was a decision that didn't make a lot of sense, given that the battery the jury believed occurred happened while Dent was trying to have sex with the victim.

Nevertheless, the outcome made him eligible to return to the team, something Coach Jimbo Fisher said he couldn't rule out. Fisher, who had been listed as a potential character witness for Dent during the trial, said he had stayed in touch with Dent as his criminal case moved forward and was "extremely happy" with how the case turned out.

"He'll text us after games, I'll text him, or during the week, just to check on him and make sure things are going well," he said at the time. "We've stayed in constant contact. Again, Greg is one of our children and you have to be there and be very supportive."

IN THE RED ZONE

S tudents at Florida State University who have suffered from sexual assault or domestic violence can seek help from the campus victim advocate's office. To get there, they must go to Champions Way and into one of those administrative buildings affixed to the Seminoles' gigantic football stadium.

It's an incongruous setting when one considers that many of the young women who come looking for support have been abused by football players. Women's advocates in Tallahassee who work with domestic violence cases said that many female students are reluctant to be seen on campus seeking out victim's services. Instead, they're left to "face enormous risk to their safety, alone with an attacker who is physically massive and habituated to physical aggression," said Meg Baldwin, director of Refuge House, a battered women's shelter in Tallahassee.

"Victims of domestic violence at the hands of FSU football players have come to us, believing that they can't go to police, can't get an injunction safely, can't complain to FSU, can't be seen anywhere near the FSU victim advocate office," she said. "None of these victims even filed a police report."

Melissa Ashton knows all about it. In the nine years she worked in the victim advocate's office, she estimated that members of the football team were implicated in at least twenty complaints of sexual assault and forty cases of interpersonal or intimate-partner violence.

Ashton spent her career standing up for people who, as she put it, "maybe don't have the same voice as I can have." After graduating from Florida State with a degree in social sciences, she went to work first for the state Department of Children and Families and then at the State Attorney's Office in Leon County, where she was a victim advocate in domestic violence cases. Ashton had been there in 2003 when the Travis Johnson case unfolded. That was the one in which Florida State's president, T. K. Wetherell, had taken the highly unusual step of personally contacting Johnson, a Seminoles football player, and his accuser, who said that other Florida State officials encouraged her not to press criminal charges.

Upon returning to Florida State in 2006—this time not as a student but as an assistant director of the victim advocate's office—Ashton was struck by the lingering sense of betrayal and disgust over the way the university had handled the Johnson case three years earlier. The staff remained upset that the university had "felt that a sexual battery was a case that could be mediated.

"They were still distraught over the case and the way everything played out," Ashton said, including that Johnson "wasn't found responsible in the student conduct hearing, and that he was not found guilty in the criminal case."

Eventually, Ashton would have her own opportunity to be upset and disgusted.

By January 2013, she had risen to the top spot in the victim advocate's office. That's where she was when Erica Kinsman came looking for help. Kinsman had identified Jameis Winston as her alleged attacker after seeing him in one of her classes and hearing his name called—weeks after the Tallahassee police had failed to come up with this same information, despite being told by Kinsman that Winston had a roommate named Chris who was a freshman football player. The police, unknown to Kinsman, had essentially shelved their "investigation" at that point.

At the victim advocate's office, Kinsman spoke to one of Ashton's staff members about what she was going through. They discussed whether Kinsman should withdraw for a semester or drop out of the race and ethnicity class she shared with Winston. Kinsman would later assert that in her meetings with the advocate's office she was never told that, under the Title IX complaint process, there were accommodations available—including requiring Winston to drop the course—to make Kinsman feel more secure. She decided to continue in the course. As for whether to pursue a student disciplinary proceeding against Winston, Kinsman held off on it because she still had not gotten back the toxicology results of her blood work on the night in question, and she was hoping they would support her belief that she had been incapacitated.

Hesitancy to proceed with a complaint was not unusual, said Ashton, noting that "the majority of survivors choose not to go through a process a lot of times based on fear." And those who do often find that the student disciplinary process does not go their way, especially if athletes are involved, since they had privileges in these matters that others did not. From where she sat, Ashton thought that players in a legal jam had "access to things that other students wouldn't," such as Monk Bonasorte, the associate athletic director who was "always with athletes who are in trouble.

"I believe that he is kind of the connection maybe to help facilitate them getting legal counsel," Ashton said.

That was certainly the case with Winston. His attorney, R. Timothy Jansen, had swooped in and shut down his client after police investigators inexplicably called Winston on the telephone, rather than confront him in person, to make an appointment to talk to him. Not surprisingly, that was an appointment Winston never kept. After that, the case went into limbo as spring turned to summer and the rookie quarterback's star started to rise with the approach of football season. Each year, the prospect of a new household name, a freshly minted hero, emerging from the Seminoles roster excited the hearts of Florida State fans on and off campus.

"It's all anyone talks about. It's all consuming for a lot of people," Ashton said, adding that she believed "an emphasis could be placed more on academics. I think it's easy to lose sight of why we're a university, and it's academics, but I think a lot of people think it's football."

Kinsman initially had not told Ashton's office the name of her alleged assailant. At some point, however, the staff member who had been counseling her mentioned to Ashton that she had figured it out, based on Kinsman's description, though Winston's name wouldn't have registered with Ashton; she was not a football fan and Winston still had not played a game for Florida State, so he was not yet the center of the FSU universe. That was about to change, however.

As Kinsman began her sophomore year in the fall of 2013, Winston was fast becoming "Famous Jameis" with his string of thrilling victories on the gridiron, rousing the passions of Seminoles Nation, who saw a possible championship on the horizon. Winston was being talked about as a likely contender for the Heisman Trophy, college football's highest honor. Florida State's campus was gripped by garnet-and-gold fever. And Kinsman was feeling more anxious than ever.

The results of her blood work had finally come back, and they were not what she had expected; they did not show her to have been legally drunk, nor did they reveal a date-rape drug in her system. This development left her even more uncertain about what to do. She met again with Ashton's office in October and shared her difficulties coping with the exaltation of Winston on campus. Her counselor suggested she try attending the next home game, on November 2, to see if she could overcome her anxiety.

Kinsman also learned something else in that meeting that gave her a jolt: a second female student had reported a disturbing sexual encounter with Winston. This was the earlier incident involving a young medical student who had sought counseling from her resident advisor, who told the victim advocate. Ashton and her staff felt Kinsman deserved to know about it. Shaken by the news, Kinsman began to cry. But she also found some new reservoir of resolve. Given that there was a second accuser, Kinsman began rethinking her hesitancy about moving forward with a complaint against Winston.

She left the advocate's office, and a week later, following her counselor's advice, she tried to sit through the Seminoles football game against Miami. As Florida State scored on the opening drive, with Winston handing the ball to Devonta Freeman, who ran it in for a touchdown, the huge crowd on Champions Way roared. Kinsman felt a rising sense of dread. She left after one quarter.

Matt Baker's kitchen phone rang with a tip that would change his life.

A young sports reporter with the *Tampa Bay Times*, Baker mainly covered high school and college games, plus the occasional NASCAR race. He had landed in Tampa a couple years earlier, after bouncing around in several newspaper jobs and internships in Dallas, Tulsa, Indianapolis, and Springfield, Missouri. A graduate of the respected journalism program at Northwestern University, Baker was well grounded in the fundamentals and could recognize a potential blockbuster story.

So his instincts were aflame on this day in November 2013 as he absorbed what the caller was telling him: Tallahassee police were sitting on a case involving Jameis Winston.

"I was writing a high school sports story of some sort, got a call out of the blue and was told that the Heisman Trophy front runner raped a girl," Baker said. "I had no clue as to whether it was true, and frankly I thought it was not."

After huddling with his editors, Baker set about trying to get a copy of the police report. His public-information request to the Tallahassee Police Department on November 8 triggered a series of increasingly worried exchanges between the city police, Florida State officials, and the university's athletic department.

After receiving Baker's request, Tallahassee police did not respond to him right away. Instead, they immediately emailed a copy of Erica Kinsman's rape complaint, which Baker was seeking, to David Perry, the chief of the Florida State University Police Department, and alerted him that a journalist was asking for it. Perry responded by inquiring about Baker's background.

"Can you share any details about the requesting source?" he said in an email to the Tallahassee police.

Chief Perry then forwarded the police report and word of the media's interest to Monk Bonasorte, the handler of messes at the university's athletic department. The Seminoles' well-oiled crisis-response machinery cranked into gear. First, Bonasorte asked whether Baker was a sports reporter; the chief said he did not know. Bonasorte then had his sports information director research Baker's background, and by the following morning, athletic department officials were circulating the reporter's résumé among themselves. He also wanted to know if there might be a legal basis for preventing release of the report by the Tallahassee police, and he told Chief Perry that, either way, he would "talk to Jimbo."

Then, mysteriously, word of Baker's request made it to Jansen, Winston's lawyer, who leaped into action. He immediately grabbed Winston's two teammates, who were the only other witnesses to his encounter with Kinsman—Chris Casher and Ron Darby— and obtained signed statements from them, corroborating Winston's denial that he did anything wrong. It's never been clear who tipped off Jansen. One possibility was Bonasorte, who exchanged at least ninety-nine telephone calls with him between November and December 2013.

In any event, having been warned about the looming publicity of the rape allegation, and therefore a possible rekindling of the investigation into it, Jansen managed to nail down crucial witnesses' testimony before the police or prosecutors even had a chance to speak to them.

On November 12—four days after Baker had filed his records request—Kinsman's aunt, Patricia Carroll, called the Tallahassee police to say that Kinsman had learned about the second female student accusing Winston of abuse. Carroll, in addition to being a concerned relative, was also a lawyer, and she had been providing advice and counsel to Kinsman for the past year as she tried to navigate her ordeal. Now, armed with this new information, Carroll was taking a more assertive role.

Her phone call to the police set off another round-robin of fretful conversations among various officials at Florida State. Tallahassee police told FSU's Chief Perry of Carroll's call, and he angrily contacted the Title IX official and dean of students at the university, Jeanine Ward-Roof, who was Melissa Ashton's supervisor. Ward-Roof came to see Ashton, saying that the chief was upset to learn that Kinsman had been told there was a second accuser.

"Jeanine said to me Chief Perry wants to know if we make it a practice of telling victims that the perpetrator has been identified in other cases," Ashton recalled. "And then that's when I found out that everyone knew and that it was going to be in the newspaper within the next couple of days. And it was blowing up."

Chief Perry's department had also been doing its own part to tamp down potential disclosure of the Winston rape allegation. In addition to the *Tampa Bay Times*'s Baker, TMZ, the online celebrity gossip site, had since gotten the same tip and called the Florida State University Police Department to ask about it. A deputy police chief, Jim Russell, responded by saying his department had no such case—without mentioning that the city police had it.

"Thank you for contacting me regarding this rumor," Russell emailed TMZ. "I am glad I can dispel that one!"

The Tallahassee police could only hold out for so long, however, on releasing a copy of the police report detailing their investigation of Kinsman's complaint. After hearing nothing for several days, Baker sent an email to the department.

"I emailed a few days ago about getting the first page (or whatever else is available) on case 12-32758," he wrote. "I haven't heard back from you all yet, so I just wanted to send a friendly follow up."

Finally, the department released the report. Heavily redacted, the document blacked out the names of Winston and Kinsman. Baker, ever the conscientious journalist, did not feel comfortable publishing a story naming Winston until he could confirm it was actually him.

TMZ, however, had fewer qualms and decided to go with it.

A few hours before the story went live online, the Tallahassee police forwarded their investigative file on Kinsman's rape complaint to the State Attorney's Office for the first time. The man in charge there was still Willie Meggs—the same prosecutor who had jailed Ashley Witherspoon's rapist, Michael Gibson, twenty years earlier. He was livid to be learning about the rape accusation almost a year after it had happened, and even angrier to discover that Jansen, Winston's attorney, had gotten a jump on him. The tip-off to Jansen, he said, allowed him to start "preparing a defense before we even know there's a case."

"Jansen," said Meggs, "knew more about the so-called investigation than we did."

There weren't many things that Tallahassee police Detective Scott Angulo did right in his investigation of Erica Kinsman's rape complaint. But he wasn't wrong when he warned early on that Tallahassee was a "huge football town" and she should think about the consequences of pressing charges against Jameis Winston.

As news of the allegation quickly spread, all hell broke loose. The narrative was as timeless as it was irresistible: the star athlete accused of wrongdoing getting preferential treatment. For many journalists, it was an opportunity to, yet again, explore the seamy underside of big-time college sports and its reliable themes of hypocrisy, fame, and corruption. Women's advocates and reformers of intercollegiate athletics seized on it to demand long-overdue change.

Sports fans, meanwhile, stared at the scene through an entirely different lens. All that mattered to them was whose side you were on—the Seminoles' or their rivals'. Football fans who hated Florida State gleefully taunted the team with reminders of scandals past, when it had earned the nicknames "Felony State" and the "Criminoles." Racism also lurked in dark corners online, where some commenters indulged in bigoted attacks on the black athlete accused of raping a white girl.

But by far, it was the supporters of Florida State football who plumbed the depths of hate, ignorance, and sleaze. In their fury over the possibility that Winston could be denied the Heisman Trophy and their team's shot at a championship could be derailed, Seminoles fans unleashed venom at anyone viewed as culpable. Online commenters called Kinsman a "lying little whore" who would "get what's coming." Her family's phone numbers were posted online, along with crudely Photoshopped pictures of Kinsman. Someone threatened to burn down her sorority house, where her sisters were demonized and one had her car tires slashed.

Ashton, too, felt the blowback, at one point filing a police report because of harassing phone calls she received at her office.

"That was just my experience," she said. "So, I know that that's minimal compared to what others experienced. And I saw what happened with social media with Ms. Kinsman's sorority. It was disgusting to the level that everything reached."

Amid the swirl of chaos and abuse, Erica Kinsman's mother came to Tallahassee and took her distraught daughter back home. She would never attend classes at Florida State again.

Journalists, too, were targeted. Matt Baker, the reporter who first got the tip about Winston, rallied after being beaten by TMZ and vigorously pursued the story, getting several scoops in the days to come. He wasn't prepared for the toxic torrent of rage, conspiracy theories, and threats that followed, beginning with a message he got from a fan saying, "FSU nation is coming for u."

"For my role in reopening a dormant investigation," he said, "Florida State fans wanted me to die of brain-eating cancer and in a car crash on my way home. They told me to jump off a bridge and get hit by a truck. They suggested I get intimate with a monkey infected with AIDS."

Baker continued: "Internet message boards tried to explain why the eleven-month-old allegation surfaced in November 2013 as the Seminoles were finishing their decade-long climb back atop college football. If Alabama coach Nick Saban didn't tip me off, perhaps former University of Florida coach Urban Meyer did. Or I wanted to sideline Winston so Texas A&M quarterback Johnny Manziel could win another Heisman. Or maybe I was sleeping with the accuser.

"And it got worse. I was covering a high school football game one night when a Twitter post popped up on my phone: 'You're a marked man . . . Say goodbye.' My wife started worrying about me at home, so she reported it to the police and the FBI. She spent that night combing through message boards, looking for other threats. Buried in the hundreds of vicious comments, she found a photo someone posted of the two of us. One of the trolls said our future children would be ugly. When I called her on the drive home, she was in tears. I didn't know what to say."

More than just fan mania was at work. Big money was at stake. In online gambling forums, sports bettors debated the impact of the Winston allegations on Florida State's odds as bowl season approached.

The first big test would be the upcoming Atlantic Coast Conference title game pitting Florida State against Duke University, and Vegas oddsmakers were busy recalibrating. A Seminoles fan on one gambling web site spread rumors that Kinsman "slept with half the town that night" and posted a picture of her. A Duke fan countered that the betting line on Winston was "innocent +275, guilty −355." Another commenter, named VegasInsider, weighed the line on Florida State versus Duke: "I'm assuming the investigation is going to conclude that they fukked consensual, he blew a load on her twat, she wanted to be his boo and he said fukk off. She got mad, cried rape, here we are. Still 29 at 5dimes."

In Tallahassee, meanwhile, Willie Meggs attempted to reinvestigate the year-old rape allegation, but quickly found that potential leads had long since expired. Chris Casher, Winston's roommate, had gotten rid of the phone he had used to videotape Winston and Kinsman having sex. Potbelly's, the bar where Kinsman said she met Winston, had recorded over security camera footage from the night in question. The cabbie who drove Kinsman and three football players back to Winston's apartment could not be identified. And Winston wasn't talking.

Meggs was disgusted at the performance of the Tallahassee police, starting with their inability to figure out Winston's identity based on Kinsman's initial description of his roommate as a freshman football player named Chris.

"There's only one person on the football team that fits that description," Meggs said. "What kind of genius does it take to find out who Chris's roommate is? The police just screwed it up."

But Meggs was also not completely sold on Kinsman's version of events. Very much an old-school lawman, Meggs, who was seventy-one, conveyed a sense of grandfatherly befuddlement at the loose sexual mores of college students.

"I drove by Potbelly's one night, must have been two in the morning. I couldn't believe it," he said, shaking his head. "Girls staggering around drunk, hanging on to each other. Guys puking over here, falling down over there. I don't know what's happened to our culture today."

Why, he wondered, did Kinsman initially tell her friend that she wasn't sure if she'd been raped? "Either you were raped or you weren't raped. How can you not be sure?" Either way, Meggs felt that something had gone wrong that evening, and "she got caught up in a mess."

Other prosecutors in his office were also disturbed. Meggs's chief assistant, Georgia Cappleman, in particular was troubled that a second female student had also complained about Winston, saying it suggested his behavior may be "a recurring problem rather than some type of misunderstanding that occurred in an isolated situation."

After a few weeks, Meggs and his team concluded there just wasn't enough evidence to charge Winston. Cappleman put it this way: "I believe that Mr. Winston cannot be convicted. I don't necessarily believe that he's innocent."

With the sports world perched on the edge of its seat, Meggs called a press conference on December 5, 2013, to announce that he was closing the investigation. Seminoles Nation was ecstatic. The good news from the prosecutor was followed a week later with word that Jameis Winston would be awarded the Heisman. And to top it off, Florida State was on its way to the national championship game in January.

Accepting the Heisman Trophy at a ceremony in New York, Winston became emotional talking about "all the things I've been through this past month.

"When you see your mom and you see your dad and they've been struggling through this whole process," he said, "and now you see a smile on their face, it comforted me."

TOUCHDOWN

When Tallahassee police initially investigated the rape complaint against Jameis Winston, detectives never learned whether the bar where Erica Kinsman said she met her alleged assailant had security cameras (almost a year later, investigators from prosecutor Willie Meggs's office discovered it had more than thirty cameras).

However, when someone swiped Mario Pender's debit card on December 19, 2013, and used it to buy shoes for $134.36, the Tallahassee police went straight to the videotape. An officer visited Champs Sports at Governor's Square Mall and pored over surveillance footage to discover who had made the purchase. It was one of three stores the police canvassed looking for security cameras for this case of petty theft.

After all, Pender—who had been arrested himself earlier that year for passing worthless checks at a Publix supermarket—wasn't just anybody. He was a Florida State football player.

A second-string running back who sat out the 2013 season for academic reasons, Pender was hardly a household name. But in this instance, the police would find a genuine evidentiary reason to be interested in his football connections: the suspect in the debit card caper turned out to be a teammate, Ira Denson, a 330-pound offensive lineman. Denson, who had been sidelined with an injury, would leave the football field early most days and return alone to the locker room, where Pender's Bank of America Visa card went missing. The card was often given to athletes who received cost-of-attendance allowances and other aid to pay for food, travel, and sundry items.

Despite being unable to play due to injuries and academic problems, Denson and Pender could still attend practices and take part in getting ready for the BCS National Championship game to be held at the Rose Bowl in Pasadena in just a few weeks. These were heady days in Tally.

Winston, freed from the threat of prosecution that had been hanging over his head, had won the Heisman Trophy and took a victory lap with an appearance on *The Late Show with David Letterman*. The blinding spotlight of the national media had trained itself on Florida State's undefeated team, and Coach Jimbo Fisher's smiling face seemed to be on every TV sportscast. The university was gearing up for huge celebrations, as well as a big payday—the collegiate conferences of Florida State and Auburn were projected to reap as much as $22 million apiece for their teams making it to the championship.

Of course, none of that money would go to the players, many of whom were from poor families and had been told they needed to sit tight and wait for their slim chance at striking it rich in the pros. Those who couldn't wait occasionally got into trouble taking gifts from boosters and stealing stuff—like Mario Pender's debit card.

Despite the diligent investigation by police, it was Pender who first pegged Denson as the likely culprit in the card theft, and on the morning of December 22 he set out to even the score. He went to Denson's apartment, not far from the Florida State campus. Denson was away visiting family, but his roommate let Pender in. While inside the apartment, Pender called Denson and told him he was taking a pair of his shoes as collateral until he repaid him for the fraudulent debit card charges. Denson replied that he would return to Tallahassee later with the money.

But Denson apparently was not ready to fold so easily. After getting off the phone with Pender, Denson texted a cousin, asking if he had a handgun. Then he texted a friend, Tarron Addison, with the same question. Addison, a convicted felon who had served time in prison and was not a football player, replied that he had a "357" and would be returning shortly from Jacksonville to where Denson was, in Madison, Florida.

The two drove back to Tallahassee in Denson's car, stopping along the way to change vehicles, before arriving at Pender's apartment complex in a white PT Cruiser belonging to a female friend of Denson's. Addison was behind the wheel, the handgun hidden beneath his seat. Denson contacted Pender to tell him he was outside with the money.

Not wanting a confrontation, Pender asked his half brother, Timothy Pruitt, to go make the exchange with Denson. Pruitt took the shoes and went down the stairs from the third-floor apartment to the parking lot, where Denson and Addison were standing beside the PT Cruiser. After placing the shoes on the hood of a parked car, Pruitt got into an argument with Denson, yelling at him for stealing from Pender. Denson and Addison yelled back. Hearing the commotion, Pender went to try to calm the situation. Going down the stairs, he noticed the PT Cruiser backing out of its parking space, and he got to the bottom just in time to see Addison pointing a chrome revolver out the driver's-side window and opening fire.

Pruitt ducked and Pender ran down a breezeway to escape the hail of bullets. One slug shattered a tenant's apartment window and lodged in a wall. Another grazed Pruitt's back. And one struck him in the head, entering his left ear and stopping behind his eye. As the PT Cruiser squealed away, Pender returned and found Pruitt moaning in pain, saying he had been shot. He and some other tenants loaded Pruitt into a car and raced to the emergency room.

Later that evening, Pender found himself sitting with a Talla-hassee police investigator, telling his story of the shooting outside his apartment earlier that day. He didn't know who the shooter was, but he didn't hesitate to name Denson and he explained the backstory of the stolen debit card that led up to the incident.

Armed with that information, police called in Denson the following afternoon, on December 23. He was read his rights and proceeded to answer questions. Detectives caught Denson making contradictory statements and confronted him with his own text messages, in which he appeared to ask about a gun before heading to meet Pender. By the end of the interview, Denson had confirmed much of what Pender had said, and even admitted that he knew Addison had brought the gun with him and that he had driven Addison back to Madison after the shooting.

"He conceded he could have gotten out of the car when he realized Addison was armed," a police account of his interview said, "but continued to Pender's apartment to settle his debt with an armed felon as the driver."

At that point, detectives essentially knew the whole story of what happened. They had enough to charge Denson, at a min-imum, with being an accessory after the fact, since he acknowl-edged helping Addison leave Tallahassee after the shooting and did not report it to the police. Instead, they drafted a warrant only for Addison, whose whereabouts were unknown, and let Denson leave.

What is more, the next day, December 24, the police issued a press release that made it appear as if the case remained unsolved. The brief statement, posted on the Tallahassee police web site, did not name anyone involved. It said the department was still investigating and sought "the public's assistance in identifying the suspect or suspects." Months would go by before either Addison or Denson were charged.

As a result, none of the few news stories published about the shooting in December connected it in any way to the Florida State football team. Thanks to the Tallahassee police, the Seminoles continued their march to the January 6 championship, safe from having to explain why two of their players were embroiled in a case of attempted murder.

As Florida State edged closer to Game Day, a festival of favorable publicity ensued, some of it cranked out by the university's public relations apparatus, but much of it organically sprung from local media outlets feeding the appetite of a community aglow with the warm, feel-good pride of a family whose loved one has hit the big time.

Leading the way was the *Tallahassee Democrat*, the city's dominant newspaper and chief cheerleader for Florida State athletics. The paper had reluctantly dragged itself into covering the Jameis Winston scandal, its editor, Bob Gabordi, practically apologizing for doing so, saying in a bizarre note to readers that it was a story "all of us wished would just go away."

"Meanwhile," Gabordi wrote, "I'll continue to cheer for Jameis Winston and the Seminoles and hope that he is cleared quickly and decisively. But I'll save a few thoughts and prayers for the well-being of this young woman, and hope you will, too."

With the unpleasantness of "this young woman" and her rape allegation safely in the rearview, the *Democrat* and other news organizations set about getting to the important stuff, like humanizing puff pieces about the football team, paeans to fan spirit, and the university's plans for a "watch party" on campus for everyone who couldn't make the trip to Pasadena. There was the touching tale of the wheelchair-bound student suffering from a condition similar to cerebral palsy, who was befriended by the football team and allowed to attend practices and pal around with the players. Coach Jimbo Fisher's own heartaches with a young son afflicted with a rare blood disease were retold, as were uplifting stories of players like Devonta Freeman overcoming long odds to climb to the top of their sport.

And then there was the web site FSUnews, a sister publication of the Gannett-owned *Democrat,* which wrote about Seminole wide receiver Kenny Shaw and his obsession with the online social media handle #3hunna. Shaw adopted it from the music of Chicago rapper Chief Keef and turned it into his own rallying cry for Seminoles fans, most of whom were oblivious to the context of its origins in street gang culture glorified in the song "3Hunna":

> I'm high I'm smoking ganja
> Fuck a tooka gang bitch I'm 3hunna

As FSUnews carefully observed, Shaw had successfully taken the meaning of the term—a sign of allegiance and support among black gang members in the urban North—and applied it to something that could be embraced by clueless Seminoles fans.

"In a strange linguistic trick, its interpretation is the same for a bunch of southern, football-loving FSU fans who are mostly white," said the article. "The gang—Nole Nation. Their weapons—their cheers. All fighting for one goal—a national championship."

Throughout the hoopla and the media's white-hot focus on Florida State and its football team, any inkling of an academic scandal would have exploded like an atom bomb. That revelation, on top of the Jameis Winston debacle, could have seriously undermined, if not derailed, the team's momentum as the championship game approached.

Yet Christie Suggs kept quiet. Nothing about her complaint of favoritism for athletes at the Dedman school, or the internal investigation it triggered, ever became public. As the holidays approached and Seminoles fever was in full boil, Christie had heard nothing more about the university's response to her concerns. Behind the scenes, her complaint was considered so sensitive that the administration had retained an outside consultant to investigate it.

Some Florida State administrators were close to panic mode. A reckoning was at hand, long overdue, with the fact that the burgeoning use of online courses at Dedman had gotten out of control and was being abused. Without much oversight, professors and aides had been deciding on their own to forgo exams and overlook plagiarism. And athletes were among the prime beneficiaries.

In early October 2013 the head of the Dedman school, Dr. Jane Ohlin, had emailed a colleague seeking help dealing with the crisis. She complained that there was "a lot of pressure" from higher-ups within the College of Business, of which Dedman was a part, "not to treat our program differently from any other dept in the COB, but we have so many online students." A dean informed Dr. Ohlin that her "online courses are under a lot of scrutiny."

"The one thing I desperately need is for there not to be any 'drama' around these online classes," Dr. Ohlin told her coworker. "We have problems with plagiarism. Problems with the answers to tests be[ing] accessible. Security is a really big deal. Any advice is most appreciated."

Meanwhile, the question arose of what to do with Christie. She had made clear to Dr. Ohlin and others that she needed full-time work, and she expected to continue in her job. Dr. Ohlin wanted to keep Christie and spoke highly of her, telling others that "her work ethic is above reproach" and she was doing "an absolutely fabulous job."

But Dr. Ohlin was overruled. The deans at the College of Business decreed that, even though Christie was certified as an online mentor—she also had two master's degrees and was pursuing a PhD in education—she could not continue in that role because she did not have enough business school credits. Dr. Ohlin tried to work out a fallback for Christie, offering her fewer hours in a lesser job that would have required her to be in the office—something she could not do.

Christie was devastated. On New Year's Eve, at home with her son, Hunter, at the tiny Panama City Beach condo she had recently rented, Christie sat down and wrote an email to Sam McCall at the inspector general's office:

> Hello Sam,
>
> I am writing to let you know that I have lost my job. I absolutely believe that I lost it due to this unfortunate circumstance with Dr. Bonn and the investigation into the football players. I expressed to you, and Carolyn Egan, my fear that this is what would happen, and it did. I really wish

you had just told me up front, when I asked, that they could fire me whenever they want and my job was not safe. I hope that in the future you will tell other people in this same situation that their job is not safe and that other people in this situation have been fired.

As a single parent . . . I have to be employed full time, and I have to work from home. I was fired from my job and then offered a "new" position where my job went from 40 hours a week to 15 hours a week which had to be done in the office. This is somewhat insulting as it is a job I obviously could not take. I was repeatedly told that my work was exemplary so I know I was not fired because of my work.

I am extremely disappointed because I believed that as long as I did good work my job was safe. I believed everyone who told me my job was safe. I would have done things very differently if I had just known. I even emailed Dr. Ohlin on October 7 asking her about my job and she said my job was secure. If I had been told the truth by even one person I would have lined up another job. I am unable to pay rent, and unable to support my child. I am desperately looking for work and feel just sick about this. I would never have let myself be without full time employment and would have a job right now if I had just known this would happen.

I hope you will just let others in my position know that this can happen. That it does not matter how good an employee you are, and to prepare for this eventuality. I am so distressed and somewhat panicked as I cannot be without a full time job to support my child.

Anyway, it occurred to me that perhaps you did not know this happens. Perhaps you were being honest. If this is the case then at least now you know and hopefully you can let other people in my situation know.

I have no idea if this situation with Dr. Bonn and the football players is resolved or not. Maybe it is resolved now and that is why they fired me now. Maybe it is not resolved and they want to ensure I will not participate in whatever is going on. I certainly do not have time for all this drama. I just want to work and take care of my child. I am not going to continue in my program and am hoping just to put all of Florida State University behind me as I move forward with my life.

I appreciate your time and wish you the best.

Happy New Year,

Christie Suggs

Ashley Witherspoon had followed the Jameis Winston drama halfheartedly. The rape accusation was too close to home for her, having gone through her own ordeal twenty years earlier at the hands of Michael Gibson. She consciously tuned it out the best she could, while still staying on top of the Seminoles' football fortunes as bowl season approached.

When the national championship game aired in January 2014, Ashley got out her garnet and gold colors and took a seat on the couch to watch Florida State take on Auburn—she was still a 'Nole, after all. But her exhilaration was tempered by what had just transpired.

The Winston rape accusation, and the way the authorities and the university responded to it, left Ashley feeling like her faith in the institutions that she believed in had been shaken. It put an exclamation point on the sad realization, evident all those years before in Coach Bobby Bowden's letter of reference for her rapist, that big-time college football was out of control. Players were idolized and could get away with anything because, in the end, winning and the money that came with it was all that mattered. She knew all that, now, and it hurt.

"We need to be addressing this early on and making these young men realize that they're accountable for their actions before they do anything stupid," she said. "Instead, we put them on a pedestal and make them think they can get away with anything, all because they can run or throw a ball. It's such a sick, broken system."

And yet Ashley and the rest of Seminoles Nation were in for a great game.

Winston—who turned twenty years old on game day—completed twenty of thirty-five passes for two touchdowns during four quarters of seesawing action. Devonta Freeman rushed for seventy-three yards and scored, but almost cost his team the game when his exuberance got the better of him and he was called for a taunting penalty after celebrating in front of the Auburn sideline.

In the end, Winston threw a come-from-behind touchdown pass with seconds left to win it, 34–31. Making the game-clinching reception was Kelvin Benjamin, one of the players in Christie's class who had handed in cut-and-pasted work and missed deadlines.

Afterwards, Coach Fisher praised his young quarterback. Making an oblique reference to the recent scandal, he said Winston showed poise despite "the atmosphere and environment" surrounding the contest.

A few weeks later, after the hullaballoo and the celebrations of the BCS championship had died down, Winston and his teammate Chris Casher were at the house they shared in Tallahassee and they wandered out to the driveway, where they started horsing around, taking selfies with their cell phones. Mugging for the camera, they laughed and sang a line together from a rap song, "On the Floor," about a man ignoring a woman's plea to go slow:

I'm not that type of guy I'll letcha know
When I see that red light all I know is go.

CHAMPIONS

I t's probably too easy to rap student athletes for their misbehavior. Young people make mistakes. Who hasn't done something foolish or regrettable in their college years that they would hate to see plastered across the front page?

In that sense, Monk Bonasorte had a point when, in his praise of Bobby Bowden, he had pined wistfully for the good old days of unheralded mischief by football players: "If you have kids, and they get into trouble, you don't tell the world. And that's the way it was back then."

Trouble is, big-time college athletics has made it impossible to ignore the bad news. By making football their public face—the "front porch," as university presidents like to say—our institutions of higher learning have placed their athletes on a stage with no curtains. It's hard to pretend you don't see the criminal behavior, the boorishness, or the academic fraud when it unfolds on your front porch right beneath the big "Welcome!" sign.

So where are the adults in these situations? Who is helping the athletes navigate not only the lows, but also the highs that come with performing under a national spotlight? Success, after all, can bring just as many challenges as failure, some of them trickier to deal with.

After winning the BCS championship, the young men of the Florida State football team found themselves on top of the world, the most wanted heroes in Florida, chauffeured in limos to the clubs of South Beach, flown by helicopter to a festival, and honored on national television. Temptations abounded.

On social media, photos appeared of players behind the wheels of Porsches and Mercedes-Benzes, stepping out of a Rolls-Royce, hanging out in bars with beautiful girls, and lounging in expensive waterfront condos. A friend of Jesus "Bobo" Wilson, a freshman wide receiver for Florida State, posted a shot of the two of them posing in a Miami jewelry store, AJ's Jewelry. In the photo, Wilson is holding a shopping bag from the store, whose owner, Anthony Machado, has his arm draped around him. The friend commented, "AJ's Get You Right Me and My Mans Copping Them Thangs," and added emoticons of little dancing diamonds.

Machado wasn't just any friendly shop owner. He specialized in selling expensive jewelry to professional athletes, and a few years earlier had been accused of giving diamonds to a member of the University of North Carolina football team, which resulted in the player being banned from the sport. A university athletics official wrote to Machado, instructing him to stay away from North Carolina athletes because an investigation "confirms you have provided impermissible benefits" to at least one of them.

Aside from the glitz and bling, there were other, more traditional rewards for being champions. There was a congratulatory call from the White House. In Tallahassee, where the crystal BCS trophy had a public viewing at the local Winn-Dixie supermarket and Walmart, thirty thousand people turned out for a celebration. City leaders adopted a resolution naming the football team worldwide ambassadors for Florida's capital city.

"This means you aren't just the greatest team in the nation or the world," gushed Mayor John Marks. "It means you're the greatest team in the whole universe."

But the excitement had to die down at some point, and then it was back to reality. The test of maturity, the duties and burdens of being a role model, comes in those times when the stadium lights dim and heroes find themselves dealing with the prosaic obligations of daily life. School. Relationships. Jobs.

Some Seminoles acquitted themselves admirably, taking time to talk to youth groups, getting back to their studies and workouts, and generally sending a positive message. Wide receiver Rashad Greene, a junior who had academic honors, was one of the players Coach Jimbo Fisher liked to take with him on media tours because he was dependable and made a good impression.

"He's very mature and a great leader, too. Affects the other guys on his team very well," Fisher told the newspaper in Greene's hometown of Albany, Georgia. "He gets it. I can look at him sometimes without even saying a word and he'll go, 'Got it,' and take care of it."

Greene, who made a key reception during the January 2014 championship game, could've left school early to join the NFL draft, but elected to stay on to complete his degree in sports management. Others dropped the pretense that they were really there for an education, withdrew, and took their shot at the pros.

But for many members of the team, getting back to reality did not go well. On the field, they turned in a lackluster performance in their first scrimmage in early spring, causing Fisher to grumble that they showed "not enough enthusiasm and excitement to be out here." Off the field, things were worse. During the rest of the year, eleven players—enough to field a starting lineup—would get into trouble, and as usual, they sometimes had help keeping it a secret.

The result was a veritable calendar of incidents, embarrassments, and arrests:

January

The 911 call came in a little after 3 a.m. on January 29. The caller told police that a man was fighting with a woman holding a baby outside their Tallahassee apartment, and he described a chaotic scene, with the man "punching her," grabbing the baby by the arm, and jumping behind the woman's car as she tried to drive away. It wasn't the first time there had been problems, said the caller, an older man who lived next door. "You can constantly hear them screaming.

"You just need to get someone out here right away because it is really bad," he said.

Officers arrived within minutes and found that the couple was back inside the apartment. The nineteen-year-old woman, K.T., denied there had been a fight, though she admitted arguing with her boyfriend and wanting to leave. The boyfriend was Tre' Jackson, an all-star six-foot, five-inch, 330-pound offensive guard on the Florida State football team, who a few weeks earlier had helped protect Jameis Winston from getting creamed by Auburn defenders as he scrambled to lead his team to victory in the championship game.

The police report of the incident—no more than a few paragraphs—raised serious questions about how thoroughly the officers investigated it. For starters, it contained a glaring inconsistency: Officer Paul Donaldson wrote that upon arriving at the door, he and his partner could hear talking inside, "but no yelling"; but then he says he spoke to K.T., who told him "it was her yelling when we were at the door," but that she was okay and didn't need the police.

Victims of domestic abuse are often hesitant to press charges, so police are trained—and in Florida required by law—to follow and document certain procedures, including seeking written statements, talking to witnesses, and forwarding a copy of their report to Refuge House, a local domestic violence shelter. The officers did none of those things, according to their report, nor did they review video from security cameras in the apartment complex that might have shed light on what happened.

The officers left and the case was closed. For good measure, Donaldson concluded his report by saying he notified his supervisor "due to the fact that it was an FSU football player." No mention of the incident appeared in the press at the time.

February

A 2014 scouting report on offensive lineman Bobby Hart said Coach Fisher was promoting him as a potential NFL first-round draft pick, and praised his agility given his huge size.

"Hart has become a very big man as his frame has filled out, and he has long arms for his height, which is already good in itself (6′4)," the report said. "He is now around 320 pounds with a very thick bubble and shows much better than average bend, particularly in the running game."

Hart, who was only seventeen when he started for the Seminoles in 2011, had physically matured into a giant by the time he took the field to help Florida State win the national championship. He towered over his girlfriend, K.F., a Florida State student who was five foot seven and 150 pounds. Unfortunately, for all his accomplishments on the football gridiron going into 2014, Hart had less reason to celebrate off the field, where his relationship with K.F. had just ended after two years of dating.

On the evening of February 9, K.F. was taking a shower upstairs in the Tallahassee townhouse she shared with a friend. When she stepped out of the shower, she found Hart waiting in her bedroom, apparently having let himself in, uninvited, through the back door. Hart was angry because K.F. had been texting other guys since they broke up, she said, and they got into an argument. After Hart refused to leave, K.F. went to her friend's bedroom and asked her to call the police.

Dispatch notes from the Tallahassee Police Department show the caller reported that Hart was "physically hitting" K.F. When Officer Joseph Smith arrived, he found Hart was gone, but K.F. appeared to have been crying and had a red mark on her arm, where she said Hart had grabbed her. Officer Smith's report concluded that the "crime of burglary w/person assaulted/battered had been committed by the suspect." However, K.F. refused to press charges and claimed Hart had not actually hit her.

"She did not want the suspect to get into trouble because he is a football player (for FSU)," the report said. "The victim refused to provide a sworn written statement and refused to allow officers to take pictures of the red mark on her left arm."

K.F. was given a "victim's rights" pamphlet and the police left. The case went unreported by the media.

March

Diehard Seminoles fans suspected something might be up when Florida State's Ira Denson didn't travel with the rest of the team to Pasadena for the national championship in January.

"When I saw that, it was a red flag," a blogger posted on Tomahawk Nation shortly after the game. "There are rumors of the latest transgression, but without documentation, I'm not comfortable publishing it because there are conflicting reports and details."

It was not until early March that Tarron Addison, Denson's friend who shot Mario Pender's half-brother Timothy Pruitt back in December following the disputed shoe purchase, was arrested. The charges precipitated a story in the local newspaper that, at long last, revealed the debit card theft and Denson's role in it. By then, the national championship was safely in the bag and the effect of the ensuing negative headlines was muted.

Asked about Denson at a press conference the next day, Coach Fisher said he was not currently on the roster, but was still enrolled in school.

"We're going to evaluate how he does," Fisher said. "He's got to continue to do well; we want him to do well academically. If he does, he does. If he doesn't, we'll have to adjust."

Ten days later, Denson himself was finally charged with the debit card theft and dismissed from the football team. It would be another week before he was also charged as an accessory in the shooting of Pruitt. Addison got thirteen years in prison. Denson was given five years' probation and sixty days at a jail work camp, to be served during summer and winter breaks from a junior college to which he had transferred after leaving Florida State.

Mario Pender, meanwhile, continued playing for Florida State until May 7, 2016. That day, police were called to a house in Tallahassee where a neighbor reported that a man had dragged a screaming woman inside by the hair. Other incidents had occurred before, the caller said. When Officer Henni Hamby got there, she heard the woman crying and pushed the door open to find Pender straddling her on the floor, his hands around her neck. The woman's right eye was bruised and there were scratches on her neck and face. The officer pulled her gun and handcuffed Pender, who—according to court records—claimed he and his girlfriend, the mother of his one-year-old child, had only been wrestling, according to court records.

"Don't you and your boyfriend wrestle?" Pender asked Officer Hamby.

Pender initially refused to get into the patrol car unless Coach Fisher was called to the scene, Officer Hamby wrote. But he eventually relented. He was charged with domestic battery by strangulation and resisting arrest. Pender, by then in his fifth year at Florida State, was kicked off the football team.

Pender's departure left the Seminoles down a man at the position of running back. Asked about Pender's arrest at a press conference, Fisher said he would have no comment on it, but quickly added, "We're OK at running back."

April

Jameis Winston just couldn't get out of his own way.

When he arrived at the seafood counter at the Publix supermarket on April 29 to collect four pounds of steamed snow crab legs and crawfish worth $28, everybody knew who he was. Twenty-year-old store clerk Justin Buis recognized the quarterback and turned to his boss to say, "Hey, that's Jameis."

But as Buis watched, Famous Jameis, the king of Tallahassee, proceeded to stroll out the front door without paying, walking past an off-duty sheriff's deputy working security, who apparently didn't notice. Buis went outside and alerted the deputy, but as the two of them looked around the parking lot, Winston was nowhere to be found. The deputy spoke to a store manager, who said her supervisors at Publix wanted to press charges.

Thus began an investigation that made Erica Kinsman's rape complaint seem like a traffic infraction by comparison. Faced with a major national chain store that didn't seem to give a damn who Jameis Winston was, two sheriff's deputies, a sergeant, and a watch commander responded to the scene of the petty theft, pulling video from twelve security cameras to piece together a second-by-second account in a thirty-four-page case file: "Camera 11, 20:53:04—Winston walks through deli area heading to produce area. Camera 9, 20:53:15—Winston enters the produce area and can be seen at the seafood counter . . ."

When deputies confronted Winston at his home, he said he had mistakenly left without paying, apologized, and said he wanted "to make it right." Rather than criminally charge him, the sheriff's office decided to give Winston an "adult civil citation" for shoplifting, requiring him to do twenty hours of community service. In a statement, Winston blamed it on "youthful ignorance" and said he took full responsibility for his "terrible mistake."

His acceptance of responsibility apparently had an expiration date. A year later, he would claim in an interview on ESPN's *Draft Academy* that the crab legs were actually a gift from a store employee and that he didn't intend to steal anything.

June

One witness said it "looked like a drug deal gone bad."

In broad daylight, several young men with guns jumped out of a vehicle in a Tallahassee apartment complex and started firing. Frightened residents ducked for cover as car windows shattered. Calls came in to the police, who scrambled a helicopter to search for the suspects.

Detectives soon figured out that three Florida State football players—Jesus Wilson, Dalvin Cook, and Trey Marshall—armed with BB and pellet guns had been horsing around with some friends, imitating the real thing but without actual firearms. Still, they'd managed to do serious property damage, scare tenants, and inflict a cost to taxpayers for an expensive helicopter mission. This was only the latest in a string of similar incidents that had begun two years earlier, all of them investigated by police without charges ever being brought.

But when the police informed the state attorney's office of this latest case of criminal mischief, they were told the prosecutors would need to "round-table" the matter among themselves before deciding how to proceed. Prosecutors chose to categorize it as disorderly conduct—a lesser charge than criminal mischief, which had carried the possibility of a felony designation depending on the cost of the damage.

The case went nowhere—and unnoticed by the media—for months until the *New York Times* learned of it and began asking questions. Shortly afterwards, in September, the police dusted it off and went back to the prosecutors, who had a change of heart. They decided to call it criminal mischief after all, though only the misdemeanor kind, thereby sparing the players the prospect of being suspended from the football team.

July

BB gun fights weren't the only mistakes wide receiver Jesus Wilson was making that summer. Around the same time as the shootout, he was stopped by Tallahassee police while riding a motor scooter that had been reported stolen by its owner, another Florida State student.

Wilson had an improbable explanation: he had borrowed it from a classmate whose last name he didn't know. That was good enough for Officer Michael Petroczky, who took the scooter but let Wilson go. Noting in his report that Wilson was a Florida

State football player, Petroczky sounded as if he was writing him a letter of recommendation, saying he "showed no signs of guilt," was "completely cooperative and calm," and offered "a plausible story" that needed to be checked out.

The officer then contacted the scooter's owner and asked to meet him on campus that evening. According to the owner—who did not want to be identified for fear of retaliation—Petroczky obviously did not want to pursue the case, and "questioned if I was mentally stable or if I had forgotten that I lent him the scooter." The officer said he was concerned about having his name on a report about an "innocent" FSU football player, the victim said.

Tallahassee police turned the case over to the Florida State University police, where it sat for weeks until the victim's father complained. On July 9, after Wilson finally confessed to stealing the scooter, he was charged with grand theft—a felony—and suspended from the team. Enter R. Timothy Jansen, the preferred lawyer of football players in trouble, who got Wilson's charge knocked down to a misdemeanor and thirty days on a county work detail—to begin after football season.

To make restitution, Wilson somehow came up with $1,000 for the scooter's owner. Where he got the money is unclear, since his mother was in civil court trying to keep her son from being evicted from his apartment, saying she was out of work and couldn't come up with the $3,139 in back rent and utilities.

September

Two weeks into the fall semester, a sophomore named Jackie was at the student union when she witnessed a fellow student engaging in the sort of offensive, moronic behavior one might expect

to find in high school, if anywhere. She tweeted her account of
what she saw:

> Well I had my first Jameis Winston sighting on campus & he
> got on top of a table in the union and yelled "fuck her right
> in the pussy"

Other students reported seeing the same thing.

> Jameis Winston standing on a table in the middle of campus
> and screaming fuck her right in the pussy

> Today I walked by some big guy who kept saying "fuck her
> right in the pussy" turns out it was Jameis Winston

> If you're wondering how my day is going so far, Jameis Win-
> ston just jumped on a table in the union and yelled "fuck
> her right in the pussy"

Winston had been mimicking a crude Internet meme. No
doubt, he thought he was being hilarious. But if anything sent
precisely the wrong signals in the wake of the Erica Kinsman
rape allegation and the rising concerns about sexual assaults on
college campuses, it was Winston's performance.

University officials, embarrassed yet again by the star making a
mess on their front porch, were forced into action. Florida State
pushed Winston out in front of the cameras to apologize for his
latest transgression, and issued its own statement calling his words
"offensive and vulgar," noting that "student-athletes are expected
to act in a way that reflects dignity and respect for others.

"As the university's most visible ambassadors, student-athletes
at Florida State are expected to uphold at all times high standards of integrity and behavior that reflect well upon themselves,

their families, coaches, teammates, the Department of Athletics and Florida State University," the school said.

The power of football was painfully obvious in what the university chose to do next: suspend Winston for only the first half of the upcoming game against Clemson University. After that punishment was widely mocked as too weak, Winston's suspension was extended for a full game. With Winston pacing the sideline and pestering Coach Fisher throughout, the team's backup quarterback managed to hang on and win it in overtime.

Crisis averted.

October

College student Ian Keith was returning home from his job at the Tallahassee Olive Garden at 2:30 a.m. when another car suddenly swerved in front of his, causing a collision that totaled both vehicles. Keith, his hand hurting from the airbag that deployed, got out and waited by the curb for the police, who arrived within minutes.

An officer approached him with a surprising question: Where was the driver of the other car? Turns out, the driver, P. J. Williams, and his passenger, Ron Darby—both starting cornerbacks for the Florida State football team—had fled on foot into the early morning darkness, leaving their wrecked Buick Century in the middle of an intersection. Making matters worse, Williams had been driving with a suspended license. Officers at the scene treated it as a hit-and-run—a criminal offense—and prepared to impound the players' car as evidence, according to an initial report of the incident.

That soon changed, however.

After about a half hour or so, Williams and Darby, along with a girl who had also been in the car, returned to the scene. Tallahassee police called Florida State University police, who, despite not having jurisdiction over the off-campus accident, sent two ranking officers to the scene. An athletic department official also arrived, as did other members of the football team.

At some point during the increasingly crowded confab in the street, the police decided not to press criminal charges, instead issuing Williams two traffic tickets; an officer took his pen and crossed out the references to impounding the vehicle for evidence of a hit-and-run that he had written earlier on his report. (Just a few weeks earlier, police had responded to a minor hit-and-run—a low-speed fender bender during the daytime—in the same area and charged the driver with a crime, even though he had turned himself in a half hour later after telling his mother what happened.)

Meanwhile, Keith, the driver of the other car, said one of the football players approached him and offered a rambling apology before a young woman with him told him to stop talking, saying, "Be quiet, you sound like you've been drinking." Even though the accident occurred at 2:30 a.m. and Williams had fled the scene, the police did not test him for alcohol, according to their report, which also appeared to minimize the accident's seriousness by indicating, incorrectly, that Keith's air bag didn't inflate.

Williams, the most valuable defensive player in the national championship game, got driven home with an athletic department official, while Keith had to hitch a ride with a tow truck. Afterwards, the accident somehow was not entered into the city's online public database of incidents. It was as if the hit-and-run never occurred, and it went unreported in the media at the time.

Late on a Friday night a couple of weeks after the hit-and-run accident, yet another Florida State football player found himself the center of attention for the wrong reasons. A young woman named Miranda Wilhelm, the pregnant girlfriend of running back Karlos Williams, publicly posted pictures of her bruised arm on Facebook, along with a disturbing statement:

> Domestic violence is NEVER okay. And I have learned why women keep secrets and [*sic*] scared to come forward. I'm ashamed to say I did the same thing. But I am ready to speak up for women in situations like myself.

After it was brought to the attention of Florida State, the university's attorney forwarded a screenshot of Miranda's posting to Tallahassee police, who opened an investigation. Miranda retained her own attorney, but she ultimately decided not to go forward with charges, telling the police in an email that it would be "best for me and my kids.

"I will, however, take help from victims advocate to help me withdrawal [*sic*] from school and start a new beginning with my life," she wrote.

Williams, meanwhile, denied through his lawyer—the busy R. Timothy Jansen—that he had done anything wrong and expressed relief that the case was over. Jansen said he had spoken to the police and wanted "no involvement in innuendo on the Internet.

"We're not giving any credence to these allegations and rumors," he said.

December

A couple of weeks before Christmas, Bobby Hart's former girlfriend K.F. went with her roommate to the Coliseum, a popular nightclub near the Florida State campus that is typically filled with students drinking and dancing. She saw Hart there with friends, and walked past without acknowledging him. Hart texted K.F.:

Quit playing w me before I fuck you up

K.F. texted back:

I call ya bluff

That prompted a barrage of texts from Hart:

Try it again and see what I come over there n do

Bring ya ass over here before I fuck you up

We supposed to b in love

Call it again

Tell luck quit playing w Ya

While K.F. was dancing, Hart approached her through the crowd. She said Hart came up from behind, grabbed her around the throat, and whispered in her ear, "What did I tell you about playing with me?" He then allegedly shook her by the neck and pushed her toward the floor before walking away.

Disoriented, K.F. took a few seconds to regain her bearings. She then walked over to where Hart had rejoined his friends and threw a drink at him. It missed and splashed a bystander, who got angry and pushed K.F. She pushed back just as a club bouncer arrived and separated them. The bouncer escorted K.F. and her roommate outside, where an off-duty Tallahassee police officer working security at the club, Jamie Martinez, was summoned. Officer Martinez later wrote that K.F. appeared "very upset" but had no visible injuries and was reluctant to provide a written statement at the scene because "she didn't want everyone watching her." However, after talking to her roommate, K.F. agreed to cooperate and said she wanted to press charges against Hart.

K.F.'s roommate backed up her account, saying she saw Hart walk up to K.F. from behind, "wrap both of his hands around her neck and start shaking her." K.F. told Officer Martinez that Hart had been violent toward her before, and according to the officer's report, he checked and confirmed the earlier incident from February in which Hart was suspected of committing burglary and battery. The officer also talked to Hart, who denied getting physical and claimed K.F. had been the aggressor; he said she had grabbed and slapped him as he walked past.

Officer Martinez then came to this conclusion: "Due to a lack of physical evidence, conflicting stories and no independent witness, no probable cause was able to be established for Hart's arrest." His report does not explain why he claimed there was no witness, when in fact K.F.'s roommate had corroborated her story and Hart had offered no one to back up his. The officer also indicated in his report that K.F. had been drinking and Hart had not, but it is not clear how he had determined that, since everyone involved had just been in a bar at 2 a.m.

This time, however, K.F. wanted to pursue the case. The next day, she and her roommate provided written statements to police, and a detective, Scott Cherry, took over the investigation. His subsequent write-up of the case began with the all-important observation, found frequently in Tallahassee police reports, that "an FSU football player was involved."

K.F. said that after she had gotten home the previous night, a red mark appeared on her neck that she said came from Hart "thrashing" her, and she took a photo of it. Investigator Cherry noted it, too, and wrote that "it was consistent with being grabbed around the neck as she stated happened." He explained to K.F. what to expect if an arrest was made, and she said she was concerned about being vilified on social media. He suggested she temporarily suspend her accounts.

"She stated that she didn't want to go through what Jameis Winston's accuser went through," Cherry wrote.

Investigator Cherry contacted the prosecutor's office, which advised that "based on information known at that point," prosecution would be declined. Cherry then reviewed the text messages that K.F. had exchanged with Hart, and he telephoned Hart, asking him to come to the police station for an interview. Hart brought along a witness—a convicted felon who had recently spent time in prison—who supported his story about being attacked by K.F. Police also contacted several bouncers at the Coliseum, who either said they didn't witness the incident or did not see Hart throttle K.F. Finally, Cherry contacted the prosecutor again, and both concluded there still wasn't enough evidence to file charges.

K.F. said she felt the police were disinclined to believe her from the start, and that Hart's football connections weighed heavily on their handling of it. On the night of the altercation at the club, she couldn't help noticing the behavior of the police officer who interviewed Hart and his friend.

"They were all laughing like three buddies at a football game," she said.

With no help forthcoming from law enforcement, K.F. went to civil court and sought a restraining order against Hart. In her application, she swore under oath that Hart had "a long outstanding history of domestic violence while we were dating" and cited five alleged incidents, including at a dance club where she said Hart physically assaulted her "and continued to try to assault me in the parking lot but was restrained by fellow teammates and friends from lunging at me as I sat in my vehicle.

"I am in fear if I don't do something," she wrote, "the violence will only escalate, as it has thus far."

A judge granted a temporary injunction, requiring Hart to stay away from K.F. and report to court for a hearing. Before that could happen, however, K.F. decided to leave the country. She enrolled in an international study program through Florida State in Europe and did not pursue the case. The injunction against Hart was dismissed in January 2015.

A few months later, Hart entered the NFL draft and went to play for the New York Giants. No account of K.F.'s allegations was ever reported in the media.

SOMETHING'S WRONG

NO. 24

Not long after Florida State won the BCS National Championship, the coveted crystal trophy left the university on a strange road trip.

In addition to making appearances at stores in Tallahassee, it popped up on display, of all places, in the lobby of the Seminole Hard Rock Hotel & Casino four hundred miles away in Hollywood, Florida, where some of the football players who earned the prize weren't even old enough to play the slot machines. The casino was one of many owned by the Seminole Tribe of Florida, including an offshore venue where gamblers can place bets on college football games and other sports.

What was the trophy doing there, given the NCAA's rigid insistence on avoiding even the remotest hint of an association between college athletics and organized gambling? The short answer is: Florida State's Seminoles owed the state of Florida's Seminoles, big time.

In the early 2000s, amid a periodic backlash against sports-team mascots and emblems deemed offensive to Native Americans, the university faced the possibility of losing its beloved Chief Osceola logo, and even the Seminoles name. A branch of the Seminole Nation out west had objected to the school's use of them, and the NCAA appeared sympathetic. But riding to the rescue was Florida's Seminole tribe, which issued a statement strongly supporting the school. The NCAA backed down, and Chief Osceola continues to gallop on horseback onto the field before games to plant a flaming spear into the fifty-yard line.

The tribe has since played a central role in redesigning the Florida State football team's uniforms, taken part in fundraising events, and even sponsors the annual Bobby Bowden Award for football players that best represent the student-athlete ideal. The university, meanwhile, started offering scholarships to students from the reservation, and allowed the tribe to help design a course on Native American history.

The relationship between the university and the tribe is held up as a model of multicultural cooperation and respect. Rarely mentioned, however, is the Seminole tribe's role as operator of one of the world's largest gambling enterprises, which, since 2007, has included the international Hard Rock brand. Its Hard Rock property in the Dominican Republic offers online sports betting, which is illegal in the U.S. The tribe's main liaison to Florida State athletics described his field of business on LinkedIn as "gambling & casinos," something that normally would preclude somebody from having a close relationship with a collegiate team. Yet he routinely has backroom access to the players and coaches and appears with them at games, special events, speeches, and award presentations.

The NCAA's strict guidelines warn student-athletes to stay away from casinos and online gambling. The association's own advertising and promotional standards, designed to prevent any association with businesses that "do not appear to be in the best interests of higher education and student-athletes," bar "establishments that include adult entertainment, gambling, sports books and the like," as well as "organizations or companies primarily involved in gambling or gaming business activities."

There is little doubt that the modern-day Seminole tribe is essentially a multibillion-dollar gambling enterprise cloaked in the trappings of Native American culture. Its tribally controlled gaming and hotel operations bring in about $5 billion a year.

It's no surprise, therefore, that the tribe owns its own aircraft—including a Bell helicopter it used to fly four top Florida State football players to an annual tribal festival a month after the 2014 BCS championship, where the players, clad in their FSU jerseys, posed with alligators and cast members of the A&E reality show *Duck Dynasty*.

It was an odd denouement to Devonta Freeman's time at Florida State.

The glow from winning the BCS National Championship had barely subsided when Freeman had a potentially life-altering decision to make: whether to stay in school or put himself up for the NFL draft.

The first junior to declare he was leaving was running back James Wilder Jr., followed by Timmy Jernigan, a defensive tackle. Another was receiver Kelvin Benjamin, who was only a sophomore but was deemed eligible for the draft because he had completed three years of post–high school education and would be twenty-four by the time he started in the NFL. Senior Kenny Shaw, a receiver, was also up for the draft.

Finally, just a couple of days before the deadline, it was announced that Devonta Freeman would be joining the exodus. Congratulations and celebratory invitations flowed in, including one for the helicopter ride to the Seminole Indian reservation, where Freeman joined Benjamin, Shaw, and Jernigan in the festivities.

Freeman soon discovered a truism experienced by many young athletes who suddenly find success: everybody wants a piece of you. Within days of announcing his eligibility for the NFL draft, Freeman posted a rant on one of his social media accounts:

> The minute people think you getting money. Watch how
> many people wanna be down. Watch how different girls
> treat you. Watch how many yes mans it be. Watch how
> people feel like you owe them something! Watch how many
> new family members you have! Watch and pay attention!
> Where was you 6 am this morning when I was working?
> Where was you when it was so dark and I was praying for a
> lil light? Huh!!! Where was you????

Luther Campbell, a.k.a. "Uncle Luke," had been there for Freeman during those dark days when others had not. He had seen promise in the budding athlete back in the Miami projects and boosted him up to where he was now, coaching and mentoring him in his father's absence, while Freeman struggled to help his mother put food on the table and buy clothes for his six younger siblings.

While running his entertainment business and coaching youth football, Campbell also positioned himself as a truth-teller about the dangers that lurked at the nexus of money and sports. He liked to inveigh against the insidiousness of sports agents, particularly those who wanted to represent black athletes, portraying them as vultures hovering on the sidelines of youth sports, waiting for a chance to swoop in. Many black families from poor neighborhoods, he said, were taken advantage of because "they are not business-savvy like some of the families of white football players.

"The agents pay a black guy from the neighborhood $500 to $1,000 to bring the player to their offices to sign the athlete," Campbell said. "It's no different from the Africans who were paid off by slave traders to identify and help capture black slaves fit for physical labor to get on a boat."

Campbell, of course, was very familiar with the world of sports agents.

Back in 2011, just as Devonta Freeman had been preparing to go to Florida State, Campbell had appeared as the keynote speaker at a symposium on sports and entertainment law. One of the panels, entitled "Family Managing an Athlete's Career," addressed issues such as "family members exploiting their children for financial gain" and "the pros and cons of having a family member as a career planner and manager."

Sitting on the panel was a lawyer and recently certified sports agent named Kristin Campbell—Uncle Luke's wife.

Kristin Campbell, who is twenty years younger than Uncle Luke, worked for her husband's business for a while before starting her own law practice specializing in sports and entertainment. She preferred not to characterize her work for young athletes as agent representation, but rather contract advice, helping them interview and choose the agent who would best manage their interests. It was the sort of arrangement that fit with Uncle Luke's theory that black athletes needed help that their white peers did not.

"Sports agents are thrown off their game when they see a foot-

ball player enter the room with an intelligent, black person representing his interests," he said. "The agents can't use their tactics
to bamboozle a potential client."

It was also a convenient business model for the Campbells.
Uncle Luke found the most talented kids, helped them along
in their sport and, when the time was right, Kristin guided
them to the next level—where the big money was. She usually
co-represented the player with another, more established agent.
Among her clients were several players who came up through
Uncle Luke's Liberty City Optimists or Northwestern High,
where he was defensive coordinator for the football team, including Durell Eskridge and Duke Johnson.

The Campbells were walking a fine line. If there was one thing
the NCAA worried about more than gambling, it was the influence of sports agents on student athletes. NCAA rules forbid
players from agreeing "orally or in writing to be represented by
an agent or organization in the marketing of his or her athletic
ability or reputation" until after they've played their last college
game. Would-be agents, "or anyone else who wishes to provide
services," are also prohibited from spending money on or giving
gifts to student athletes.

There is no evidence that the Campbells broke these rules.
But the proximity of Luther Campbell to young athletes who
later wound up hiring his wife to represent them raises questions that do not appear to have ever been asked, let alone exam-
ined closely, by the NCAA. Certainly, considering the Campbells'
close association with Devonta Freeman—who has described
Uncle Luke and Kristin as family—it's fair to ask when, exactly,
conversations took place about young Devonta's future plans and
who would represent him.

Because, as it turned out, he was Kristin Campbell's first
major client.

In the 2014 NFL draft, Freeman hit the jackpot, landing a four-year, $2.7 million contract with the Atlanta Falcons and reaping a $475,000 signing bonus. He was his typical carefree self, telling the press that as long as his mother, Lorraine, was happy, he was good.

"Me personally, I don't want nothing," Freeman said. "I promise you. I can't tell you one thing I want. It's just good to know I ain't got to want for nothing, and I can take care of my family."

Freeman did get one thing he had long sought.

Just as his first season with the Falcons was about to start in September 2014, Freeman's teammate, cornerback Jordan Mabin, was cut from the roster. That freed up the jersey number—24— Freeman had wanted ever since his aunt Tamekia had died at that age back when he was only fourteen.

He was wearing No. 24 in his first professional game when he caught a pass and bulled his way thirteen yards to set up a key first-and-goal, prompting the TV announcer to exclaim, "What an effort!

"If you're a rookie in this league and you want more playing time," he said, "play with will like that!"

Down on the field, Freeman had been flattened by three defenders, but he popped back up on his feet. A proud Uncle Luke wasted no time posting on his Instagram page an image of Freeman, with the message, "Take this to every team who pass on him in the draft." That was followed by more photos, one of them of another player he'd mentored who was also a client of Campbell's wife, as well as a picture of a boy who was still with Campbell's youth team. Uncle Luke clearly had high hopes for him.

"He's 6′5, play for the Liberty City Optimist," he wrote. "He's in the 8th grade."

GETTING A BOO$T

The windowless interview room at the Leon County Sheriff's Office in Tallahassee has seen all manner of criminals and miscreants pass through, often on their way to prison for violent crimes. On October 1, 2014, the lengthy roster of charges for the thirty-two people booked into the jail that day included child abuse, robbery, and assault with a deadly weapon.

And then there was the white-haired sixty-four-year-old man dressed in button-down shirt and khakis, sitting quietly in the interview room, looking at his smartphone, his eyeglasses resting on the table in front of him. He could easily have been mistaken for a defense attorney or insurance investigator. But Sanford Lovingood was a suspect.

Lovingood had been the chief financial officer of the Seminole Boosters for twenty-five years, in charge of handling the millions of dollars that flowed into the organization. In addition to cash, stock, and other gifts from wealthy donors, the group collected revenue from skybox rentals and concessions at the football stadium, as well as media rights, licensing, and royalties related to Seminoles sports. In 2013, the Boosters had assets totaling $264 million.

So, with all that cash sloshing around, who was minding the store? Not Florida State University.

The Boosters are largely independent of the school, run by their own board of directors that sets policy, hires staff, and approves budgets mostly as it sees fit, though it works closely with university officials on fundraising and spending for athletics. In meetings of the university's board of trustees, then-president Eric Barron never challenged the Boosters in any meaningful way, despite occasional concerns about a general lack of accountability. During a board discussion in 2011, Dr. Barron mentioned that his office was supposed to approve the Boosters' spending each quarter, but "I've never gotten a quarterly expenditure approval from the Boosters." Rather than insist that they start submitting them, Dr. Barron recommended that the group's bylaws be changed so that his approval was no longer necessary.

Into this void of outside monitoring, someone like Sanford Lovingood could maneuver to steal close to $1 million with no one noticing for years. The barn doors had been left wide open, and as a repentant, comically self-critical Lovingood characterized himself during his confession to a detective in the sheriff's interview room, "Here comes Mr. Dumbshit."

The detective, Jared Lee, handed Lovingood a soda and took a seat.

"Thank you," Lovingood said. "You need to put some Jack Daniel's in this."

Lee had just talked to several officials of the Seminole Boosters, who were still in shock that such a well-known fixture of the group had been embezzling, under their noses, for almost four years. An audit had finally detected some discrepancies in accounts, prompting a hastily arranged, if awkward, invitation for Lovingood to join his colleagues for lunch. There, he was confronted with the evidence and he admitted the theft.

"Guys, I did it," he said. "I ain't gonna hide nothing from you."

Now, Detective Lee was asking him to go through it in detail.

"People make stock donations to the Seminole Boosters," Lovingood patiently explained. "It goes in this account. We sell the stock and the cash goes in this account and every so often we would draw that money out and put it over in our operating account. And I was a signature on that account. Had been for years. And I began to write checks to a corporation I am involved in and then taking money from that corporation and putting it either in TD Ameritrade or my personal account."

According to Lovingood, he started stealing the money to cover trading losses in his brokerage account, but things got out of hand. Using a pen and paper, Lovingood drew a diagram for Lee, showing the process by which he wrote ninety-seven checks and made a wire transfer totaling $870,000 from a Boosters account for his own use.

"Here's my question," Lee said. "And the obvious question, being, 'Why?' "

"Because I'm fucking stupid."

"Your friends are saying—they're your friends—you're an intelligent guy."

"Because I would lose money and I would say, 'If I can just put it back in there, I will be okay,' you know?"

"Did you think you would be able to put it back?"

"What I was planning on doing is—I knew I could not proba- bly make restitution to the Boosters in my lifetime," Lovingood said. "What I was planning on doing eventually was gifting back some of my estate at my death."

Lovingood never got the chance. He was charged with racke- teering, grand theft, and money laundering, pleaded no contest, and was sentenced to eight years in prison. Among the character witnesses who testified on his behalf was a former assistant coach of the Florida State football team.

As for the Boosters, their president, Andy Miller, issued a statement reassuring donors that an internal review had "verified that all gifts and transfers were properly credited to the appropriate donor accounts." Lovingood, however, had made clear in his confession that he had been stealing donations. Asked about the source of the money, he replied, "All of that is donor."

Such damaging revelations would have upended many a nonprofit group and spurred demands for an outside inquiry into its lack of governance. After all, the Seminole Boosters are legally a charity, registered as a tax-exempt 501(c)(3) organization with the Internal Revenue Service to "promote the education, health and physical welfare of the students of Florida State University." But the Boosters emerged from the scandal largely unscathed. Donors and Florida State fans rallied around and the whole unseemly episode was quickly left behind.

That is because, in the world of college sports, booster organizations are the equivalent of "too big to fail" Wall Street institutions whose collapse is just too painful to contemplate. As Dr. Barron said during the board of trustees discussion back in 2011, "I don't know what we'd do without them."

Left unsaid was that booster groups and nonprofit foundations that support universities are useful in ways that college presidents prefer not to talk about in polite company. The private money they oversee comes in handy for questionable tasks that the schools themselves can't, or won't, dirty themselves with. The Seminole Boosters, for instance, paid more than $500,000 to buy out the contract of Jeff Bowden—former coach Bobby Bowden's son—when the university wanted to get rid of the football offensive coordinator in 2006. The Boosters also paid about $70,000 in legal fees for the university to challenge the NCAA's vacating of Coach Bobby Bowden's victories because of the *Apollo 13* academic scandal.

Ten years later, the Boosters would be called upon again to help tidy up an even bigger mess: fallout from the Jameis Winston rape allegation.

In olden times, booster groups might have been more akin to a glee club, but today they have a far more important mission: making it easier for cash-strapped schools to compete in the money race for coaches and facilities, while also skirting their own rules on prohibited expenditures. Using private donations, for example, is a way to get around state caps on salaries for public university employees and cover the cost of alcohol when athletics department employees travel on business.

In an environment of declining state support and rising costs, public universities in particular find themselves increasingly reliant on wealthy boosters. Colleges saw the total value of private donations for athletics rise at a much higher rate—53 percent— in the five years preceding 2014 than donations overall, which rose by 22 percent. But the growing practice of outsourcing the financing of intercollegiate athletics has spurred criticism that boosters are sometimes allowed to influence the shape of athletic programs, including the hiring of coaches and recruiting of players.

At the University of Texas, booster Joe Jamail was a towering figure for decades, showering tens of millions of dollars on his beloved alma mater, including endowing a fund that helped pay the chancellor's salary. A legendary tort lawyer who got rich bankrupting Texaco with a $10.5 billion jury verdict for Pennzoil in the 1980s, Jamail loved Texas Longhorns football almost as much as courtroom duels. His name adorns the football field and other facilities on the university campus, where not one, but two statues of the man have been erected.

And Jamail, who died in 2015, did not hesitate to throw his weight around. When there was talk of replacing the longtime football coach Mack Brown—his friend and client—the feisty old trial lawyer said Brown should be okay because Jamail and another big booster, Red McCombs, supported him, "and that's a lot of money." As for angry Longhorns fans who had threatened to knock down Jamail's statues on campus, he had this to say: "Tell them to send me my money back, and then they can pull the statues down. I don't know who the hell those fucking crybabies on the Internet are. Could be Aggies or the Taliban, for all I know. Or fucking al Qaeda."

Beyond the gridiron, there are other reasons to worry about the growing power of boosters and the groups they fund.

After University of Central Florida football player Ereck Plancher collapsed and died following practice drills, his family wanted to sue the school for negligence. They soon discovered that would be harder than they thought, because the university basically claimed it did not run its own athletic department. Rather, managerial control had been shifted to the privately funded UCF Athletics Association, which, according to laws passed by the state legislature, shared little information with the public, including the identities of donors who gave it millions of dollars. As university athletic director Kenneth Tribble said in a deposition during the lawsuit, the secrecy came in handy when paying coaches "without having it, you know, become public."

The end-run around transparency is but one example of how booster organizations, and the public universities that benefit from them, are looked after by political allies. For instance, tax-exempt groups normally must file an annual report, called a Form 990, with the IRS, detailing their finances, including salaries paid to their executives and the names of their largest donors; all of the information, except for the donors, is public and can easily be found online.

But some schools have taken to making it more difficult to learn what their booster supporters are up to. When the Crimson Tide Foundation was created in 2004 to raise money for the University of Alabama's legendary football team and other athletic endeavors, it filed a Form 990 for its first year of operation, showing it had $33.9 million in assets and paid its president $330,000.

That was the last Form 990 it ever filed. Thereafter, the foundation was declared to be a "blended component unit" of the state-run university, thereby exempting it from the requirement that it disclose its finances in a public report to the federal government. You can still find some basic information—such as the fact that by 2013 the foundation's assets had ballooned to $132 million—but you need to dig through a sixty-five-page financial report for the entire University of Alabama, which does not reveal individual salaries and other details found in a Form 990.

Another detail not found in the financial report is that the Crimson Tide Foundation spent $3 million to buy the 8,759-square-foot home that Alabama football coach Nick Saban lives in. Apparently, the $7 million salary paid to Saban—the highest-paid public employee in America—wasn't incentive enough for him to stick around.

The Seminole Boosters' influence begins at the top. Florida State president Eric Barron's employment contract said the Boosters would contribute to his pay and benefits, as well as deferred compensation tied to performance goals that include maintaining a strong athletics program. Four current and former members of the Boosters board served on the university committee advising Florida State on its search for a successor to Barron, who left in 2014 to become president of Penn State.

Though not legally a department of the university, the group has offices at the stadium, its employees use Florida State email addresses, and it exerts significant influence over the athletic program—even effectively controlling a portion of its budget. It funds roughly $7 million a year in operational costs for the athletic department, as well as numerous capital projects, including housing for student athletes and stadium improvements. To bypass NCAA restrictions on boosters paying coaches directly, the Boosters funnel millions each year through the FSU Foundation, which in turn directs the cash to the athletics department for that purpose. In its financial statements, Florida State acknowledges the shell game, saying it establishes "institutional control as prescribed by the NCAA" over the money.

While occupying a central role in Florida State's athletics program, the Boosters have long been run by powerful political and business figures in the state capital. While it is perhaps not surprising that a capital city–based athletics program like Florida State's would enjoy the support of the political establishment, the Seminole Boosters are plugged in to the Tallahassee power structure in a variety of useful ways. Its board has traditionally been populated with movers and shakers, including David Rancourt, a former deputy chief of staff to Governor Jeb Bush. Rancourt cofounded a powerful lobbying firm, Southern Strategy Group, which has several members on the board of coach Jimbo Fisher's family charity, Kidz1stFund.

The Boosters have teamed up with a Florida State athletics social club, Old School, whose fundraisers with Dr. Mark Bonn from the Dedman School of Hospitality and Fisher's Kidz1st-Fund have attracted influential Tallahassee figures. One of their auction-and-golf-tournament events featured the chief of the Tallahassee Police Department firing a shotgun for the ceremonial start. Up for auction was a private dinner at a booster-run club with the speaker of the state House of Representatives, billed as an "exclusive experience to dine with one of Florida's political heavyweights." Winners also got to spend a day with the Broward County sheriff to learn how "law enforcement keep the peace."

With so little outside oversight, coupled with the influence it wields, the Boosters freely engage in business deals affecting the university, but with little accountability to officials there. For instance, the group launched a $27 million, tax-subsidized real estate development called College Town on behalf of Florida State. The project, a mix of retail and residential development, was riddled with potential conflicts of interest that most likely never would be allowed had it been a state project: nine members of the Boosters board had a personal investment stake in College Town through a limited liability company created for that purpose (although they abstained from voting to approve the project), and boosters were given the contract to develop and build it.

One reason the university does not have a lot of incentive to police such matters is because the cash raised by the Seminole Boosters comes in handy in a crisis—such as when it is faced with a lawsuit with a price tag approaching $3 million.

After leaving to finish college elsewhere, Erica Kinsman had to return to Tallahassee in December 2014 to testify at the student code of conduct hearing that had been called to consider the rape accusation against Winston. The belated decision to hold the hearing was the culmination of a long, tortured journey that saw Florida State University become the focus of nationwide anger over the mishandling of sex crimes on college campuses in general, and favoritism toward athletes in particular.

In defending itself against the criticism, the university only made matters worse.

Melissa Ashton, who ran the campus victim advocate's office, was shocked when the office of the university's general counsel— Carolyn Egan, the same lawyer who handled Christie Suggs's whistle-blower complaint—demanded to see her file on Erica Kinsman before it was released to Kinsman. Ashton believed the policy was that such records were supposed to be confidential and available only to victims or their representatives.

Egan's office insisted it only wanted to review them before their release and assured Ashton that it was proper. But when information in those records later wound up being cited in a statement issued by the university, defending its conduct in the Kinsman case, in which FSU recounted efforts by the victim advocate's office to help her, Ashton said she regretted caving in to the university's lawyers.

"Turning them over made me extremely uncomfortable," she said. "I questioned it. I questioned it when I was doing it. I questioned after I did it, 'Should I have done it?'"

Moving ahead with a student code of conduct hearing for Winston was another attempt by Florida State to counter the impression that it had failed to handle the case properly. Here again, there was controversy. The university chose an unorthodox procedure, going outside the school to pick a panel of three retired jurists and allowing lawyers for Winston and Kinsman to each strike one of them, leaving the third to oversee it: Major Harding, a seventy-nine-year-old former chief justice of the state Supreme Court.

Harding presided over a closed-door hearing in December 2014 that included testimony and evidence from both sides. Winston at first exercised his right to not speak. However, after Harding pressed him to explain whether Kinsman had verbally or physically given her consent to have sex, Winston consulted with his lawyer and then answered.

"Both, Your Honor," Winston said. "Verbally and physically."

"And what did she say and what did she do?" asked Harding.

"Moaning is mostly physically. Well, moaning is physically. And verbally at that time, Your Honor."

"Well," Harding said, "that was during the sexual encounter?"

"Yes, Your Honor," said Winston.

That was the extent of Winston's testimony.

The atmosphere surrounding the hearing had uncanny echoes of the previous year, when the fate of Winston—and the undefeated Seminoles football team—had hinged on the outcome of the belated prosecutor's investigation in December 2013, just weeks before the college playoffs. This time around, events were unfolding almost exactly the same way, with another judicial cliff-hanger coming amid an undefeated season on the eve of the critical Rose Bowl game that would determine whether Florida State again competed for the national championship.

On December 21, Harding's decision was announced: the differing versions of what happened in Winston's bedroom were "irreconcilable," and he couldn't find enough evidence to conclude that Winston had violated the student code.

"In light of all the circumstances," the retired judge said, "I do not find the credibility of one story substantially stronger than that of the other. Both have their own strengths and weaknesses."

It was hardly a ringing exoneration, but FSU Nation chose to take it that way. Jubilant fans cheered as Winston and the rest of his team prepared to meet Oregon in the Rose Bowl. Kinsman's lawyers expressed consternation at Harding's finding, arguing it ignored the significance of Winston's strained explanation of how Kinsman had supposedly given consent.

"It's all about a football game ten days from today," said attorney Baine Kerr. "It turned out to be just a predetermined whitewash to keep a guy playing football."

History would not repeat itself, however. Florida State was humiliated in the bowl game, losing 59–20, and fell short of making it to the championship game. Deciding not to press his luck any further at Florida State, Winston left before finishing school and entered the NFL draft, where he was the No. 1 pick, landing a spot with the Tampa Bay Buccaneers. Kinsman, meanwhile, sued the university, claiming it failed to properly investigate her sexual assault allegation. She also sued Winston separately, leading him to countersue her for defamation.

After a year of litigation in U.S. District Court and $1.7 million in legal fees, Florida State made the decision to settle the lawsuit with Kinsman. While not admitting wrongdoing, it offered her $950,000 and agreed to continue reforms to the way it handled Title IX cases that had been put in place after the allegations against Winston became public. But in agreeing to settle, Florida State proved it was still in denial.

Under its new president, a former state politician with no academic experience named John Thrasher, the university issued a mean-spirited statement making it clear that the school was only settling to save money and suggesting that Kinsman's lawyers were slated to keep $700,000 of her settlement—something they denied. It was a deeply troubling performance by a public university at a moment that demanded grace and healing.

Thrasher, who kept on his desk a photo album with pictures of his family's visit to FSU shortly after he became president—including shots of Winston posing and signing autographs with them—also chose to leave out a couple of important facts about the settlement. It came shortly before depositions were scheduled for some key figures, including Monk Bonasorte, the athletic department's in-house fixer, and Chris Casher and Ron Darby, Winston's two friends who were with him the night he had sex with Kinsman. By agreeing to fork over close to a million dollars, Florida State avoided potentially damaging testimony.

Also not explained was how the settlement was being paid. State insurance covered the payment to Kinsman and $421,000 of the school's legal expenses. Where did the remaining $1.3 million for attorney's fees come from?

The Seminole Boosters.

The Boosters insisted that the money would not come from donors, but rather from operational revenues, such as licensing fees. But as the Sanford Lovingood case had already demonstrated, the Boosters could not be counted on to be completely transparent in their assurances about how donor money was used—or misused.

Not that most donors would likely have cared if their cash went to clean up Jameis Winston's mess. After all, he had gotten them the coveted crystal trophy, and that was all that really mattered.

CHRISTIE

Tidewater Beach Resort is a gigantic sand-colored box of condos looming above the gulf surf in the Florida spring-break destination of Panama City Beach. Amenities include a tiki bar, community hot tub, and proximity to local nightlife. It's the sort of place that attracts young partiers and tourists looking for an affordable vacation. Maybe the occasional retired snowbird.

One would not naturally expect to find an aspiring PhD student living alone there with her twelve-year-old son. But that's where Christie Suggs was spending her days at the start of 2014, in a cramped one-bedroom rental unit near the elevator.

The decision to leave Florida State without earning her doctorate was deeply painful. She had spent years and borrowed tens of thousands of dollars, and yet would end up settling for an education specialist degree—one step short of what she had wanted. Christie expressed her disappointment to her friend Melissa Isaak, saying she couldn't continue without the steady work provided by her Dedman job and had grown weary of the anxiety caused by her complaint about the football players.

"I can't stress enough how important this PhD was to her," said

Isaak. "Next to her son, Hunter, it was the single most important thing in her life."

Christie remained angry about what happened with her job at Dedman, convinced that fallout from her complaint about the football players had something to do with it. She talked about suing the university. But in the end, she decided to let it go and try to move forward.

Christie's life only became more difficult as the year wore on. She struggled to find part-time jobs, her only consistent income being the $19,400 she made from teaching online courses for Kaplan University. Money was tight. Her biggest monthly expenses, aside from rent and groceries, were lunch money and school clothes for Hunter. Her clunker car was worth only about $1,100. Luckily, she spent little on gas because her online jobs could be performed at home.

As pressure mounted, she fell back on her past career in social work and started looking for counseling jobs. She went on food stamps and reluctantly sought a child support enforcement order against her estranged husband.

Christie's physical and mental health worsened over the coming months. Friends thought she was depressed. She had suffered from depression in the past, but now the stress was becoming apparent in other ways as well. She gained forty pounds and developed back problems that required surgery. In early October, her mother, Margie, agreed to come down from Alabama and help out while Christie recovered from the operation.

Christie had insisted on working even while recuperating, propped up in bed with her laptop. On October 9, she told her mother she felt tired and would take a nap, while Margie took Hunter out to a restaurant. They returned later to find Christie lying on the bed, clad in her purple nightshirt and pajama pants, with one leg dangling over the side. Not wanting to awaken her daughter, Margie went to gently lift Christie's leg back onto the mattress. Immediately she saw that something was wrong. A small trail of blood seeped from Christie's nose. She wouldn't wake up.

Christie Suggs was dead at age forty-eight. The medical examiner would later rule her death an accident, a toxic combination of some of the twelve different prescription drugs in her system for pain, depression, and anxiety.

Friends and family gathered four days later for Christie's funeral at the Lakeview Baptist Church in Auburn. Afterwards, Margie, distraught and searching for answers, turned to Christie's friend Melissa with a question.

"Do you think the football players did this?" she said.

AFTERWORD

Certain people would not talk to me for this book. One of the downsides of having already published critical stories about a topic is that when you later try to interview somebody about it, they can see you coming a mile away. They think they know what your game is, and they don't want to play.

Jameis Winston, Luther and Kristin Campbell, and Michael Gibson's family ignored my repeated requests, some of them made in writing, to speak to them. Others, including Bobby Bowden, T. K. Wetherell, and the Seminole Boosters, politely begged off.

Meanwhile, courageous souls like Ashley Witherspoon, whom you might not expect to open up about their experiences, agreed to share their stories. Some wanted to remain anonymous. Several victimized young women spoke movingly about what they went through, first at the hands of abusive athletes and, later, uncaring authorities. A former police officer explained what it was like trying in vain to hold football players accountable for crimes. A sports agent told me about the corrupting influence of boosters.

As I made the rounds seeking comment and insight, I invariably heard from defenders of Florida State, who argued—usually off the record and in high dudgeon—that I had it all wrong. Mine was an elite, northeastern media viewpoint, they said, bent on caricaturing Southern ways and unfairly smearing a respectable institution for the sake of titillating headlines. Yes, this line of thinking went, Florida State had taken its lumps like a lot of schools, but the Jameis Winston scandal was overblown and the university didn't get credit for all the good things it did.

But wait a minute, I'd say, what about the Florida State people I heard from who believed the opposite was true? There were the parents who feared for the safety of their daughters on campus. The professors who felt marginalized and intimidated by the power of athletics. And the whistle-blowers desperate to draw attention to what they saw as the corrosive and misguided emphasis on an out-of-control football program.

It was one of these people who first mentioned Christie Suggs. From the start, Florida State University resisted giving me information about her complaint, taking the better part of a year to produce records I sought, and even then, withholding key pieces of information on the grounds that it was exempt from public disclosure.

What the university did provide was not always accurate. At one point, it released to me a statement by Dr. Mark Bonn, Christie's boss at the Dedman school, saying, "Our online beverage courses were never cancelled." This, despite an extensive email trail between administrators showing they were, in fact, cancelled for the fall of 2013, in part because of concerns about academic integrity. Questioned about this, Florida State subsequently acknowledged it was true, but insisted it "had nothing to do with Ms. Suggs or her report."

So what about that report? What did the university do to

address it, and what did it conclude? I repeatedly asked for records related to the report, and was denied. Instead, the office of the legal counsel, Carolyn Egan, issued a statement: "Regarding Ms. Suggs and her report, we are unable to provide any documents regarding that investigation or its outcome without jeopardizing the privacy of students involved."

It's possible that the conduct Christie complained about—as plainly inappropriate as it was—did not rise to the level required to trigger an investigation by the National Collegiate Athletic Association. And that's really the biggest concern for major college sports programs, since the consequences of such inquiries can be grave in terms of penalties and bad publicity. The NCAA generally permits institutions to investigate academic fraud allegations internally and decide whether it violates NCAA rules. By doing so, there is an inherent conflict of interest.

Dr. Gerald Gurney, a senior associate athletics director for academics at the University of Oklahoma and past president of the Drake Group, which advocates for academic integrity in college sports, said the NCAA has been stepping back from policing academics on campuses and "doesn't want to deal with the widespread cheating that schools tolerate to keep athletes on the field. The NCAA simply tries to avoid public scrutiny of educational scandal."

In 2016, the NCAA started employing an elaborate "academic misconduct analysis" to determine if it will get involved in a case. A key factor is whether the alleged misconduct resulted in an athlete being improperly certified to play. In the case of football players identified by Christie Suggs, that's impossible to know without access to their grades and other records.

"Clearly, there are academic integrity issues here that apply to NCAA rules, but the key is whether it affected certification of eligibility," Dr. Gurney said. "I would suspect that it is an impermissible academic assistance problem, but I'd need more information."

Alas, such information is not forthcoming. The NCAA declined to comment, saying it "would be best for you to follow up with the school on this matter." I did, and all Florida State would say is that it "engaged a highly regarded outside entity to investigate the issue and the entity concluded no wrongdoing on the part of Dr. Bonn or anyone else."

Case closed.

The path to reforming college sports is so steep that most people in a position to attempt it don't even bother (see "Suggs, Christina Lynn" if you want to know what happens to people who try).

Vested interests who benefit from the status quo include big media and corporate sponsors, university presidents and coaches, fans and alumni. Congress loves college sports, as the IRS found out in its futile attempts to show that the tax-exempt emperor has no clothes, and so do state legislatures and local businesses that are pilot-fish trailing alongside the whale of big-time football and basketball programs.

What are the options for bringing about change? There are a few—including, against all odds, limiting the tax breaks accorded to college athletics. One of President Barack Obama's budget proposals took a stab at that. It would have curtailed the tax deduction for booster donations tied to the purchase of stadium seats and luxury boxes. Though it didn't get anywhere, even suggesting such a measure was an unlikely step in the right direction, in that it would impose change in the place where college sports is most sensitive: the wallet.

It is money, after all, that fuels the engine of the corporate-athletics complex. Other tax initiatives could include fragmenting the tax treatment of revenue flowing through athletic departments, so that broadcast fees—one of the largest sources of commercial revenue—are taxed as "unrelated business income," given their almost complete disassociation from the tax-exempt educational mission of the university. In addition, the IRS or Congress could drop the absurd classification of corporate sponsorships as something other than advertising, which is taxable.

Other possible avenues for reclassifying sports-related revenue would be to restructure the relationship between universities and their athletic departments. Considering that many of them already function as autonomous fiefdoms, why not cut the umbilical cord completely so they cannot cling to the tax-exempt protections of their in-name-only affiliation with the university? This, again, would open the sports programs to taxation, limit profits, and take some of the wind out of the sails of the entire enterprise.

Ultimately, however, it may take the creation of something like a minor league for football and basketball players coming out of high school, similar to what exists now in baseball. Many baseball players go straight from high school into a minor-league farm system by signing a contract that guarantees them college tuition, sometimes even if they end up washing out as a player.

But what is the likelihood that any of these changes will come about? The hurdles, financial and cultural, are enormous. Financially, there is little incentive for pro football and basketball leagues to incur the expense of establishing farm systems, when they have the NCAA providing that service for them. As a top official of one of the Power Five college athletic conferences told me, "The NFL and NBA have us exactly where they want us." In

the case of football, there are also concerns about young players coming out of high school having the physical ability and
skill set to perform at the professional level, even in a minor-
league setting.

Then there is the inescapable reality that college sports have
become as much a part of America's cultural DNA as pizza and
reality television. When the president of the United States makes
a show of picking his brackets for the NCAA men's basketball
championship, fundamentally altering the sport won't be easy. It
would literally take an act of Congress to impose changes to the
tax code and the university–athletics relationship, and, again,
the political incentives are lacking.

It may be left to the courts to hack away at the status quo. His-
torically, the judiciary has been as willing as the rest of our public
institutions to give big-time college athletics a pass, issuing rul-
ings supporting the increasingly frayed notion that it is a defen-
sible component of schools' educational mission. But recently,
fissures have appeared in this legal bulwark, notably a federal
judge's decision—later overturned on appeal—opening the door
to college athletes sharing in the profits from the commercial
use of their names and likenesses. Other lawsuits pushing similar
claims are pending. This slippery slope into the professionaliza-
tion of student-athletes has the potential to transform college
sports, by lifting the facade of amateurism and forcing universities, and the public, to confront the reality before them.

For the reality is this: If student-athletes are indeed to be
treated as professionals, then are they really students? And if not,
then what place do they have on campus?

NOTES

PREFACE

ix   **bankruptcy filed by the sports agent**: Petitioner John T. Lounsbury, Case No. 96-34290, U.S. Bankruptcy Court, District of Connecticut.

xi   **all NCAA corporate "champions"**: "Corporate Champions and Partners," NCAA, last modified November 16, 2016, accessed December 13, 2016, http://www.ncaa.com/news/ncaa/article/2011-02-25/corporate-champions-and-partners.

xii   **revenue of $8 billion**: Paula Lavigne, "College Sports Thrive Amid Downturn," ESPN, May 1, 2014, http://www.espn.com/espn/otl/story/_/id/10851446/sports-programs-nation-top-public-colleges-thrived-economic-downturn-earning-record-revenues.

xiii   **"darkest blot upon American college sport"**: Howard J. Savage, Harold Woodmansee Bentley, John T. McGovern, and Dean Franklin Smiley, *American College Athletics*, Bulletin No. 23 (New York: Carnegie Foundation for the Advancement of Teaching, 1929).

xiii   **"sanity had to be restored"**: Knight Foundation, *Reports of the Knight Foundation Commission on Intercollegiate Athletics, March 1991–March 1993* (Charlotte, NC: Knight Foundation Commission on Intercollegiate Athletics, 1993).

xiii   **"As we callous our collective consciences"**: Wally I. Renfro, email message to Mark Emmert, October 17, 2010.

xv   **"It got very emotional"**: Richard Miller, interview with author.

xv   **series of lengthy reports on spending**: Joint Legislative Audit and

Review Commission, *Review of Non-Academic Services and Costs at Virginia's Public Higher Education Institutions: Report to the Governor and the General Assembly of Virginia* (Richmond, VA: September 2013).

xv **two highest-paid public employees**: "NCAA Salaries: NCAAF Coaches," *USA Today,* http://sports.usatoday.com/ncaa/salaries/.

xvi **a blockbuster story**: Walt Bogdanich, "A Star Player Accused, and a Flawed Rape Investigation," *New York Times,* April 16, 2014.

xvi **$200 million in assets**: Seminole Boosters, Inc., *Financial Statements and Other Financial Information: Years Ended June 30, 2013, and 2012 with Report of Independent Auditors.*

xvii **Take Dr. Eric Barron**: "President Eric J. Barron," PennState Office of the President, http://president.psu.edu/biography.html.

xvii **"We have this expectation"**: Gary George, "Florida State Seminoles BCS National Champions: Dr. Eric J. Barron" (interview with *Inland Valley News*), posted on January 8, 2014, https://www.youtube.com/watch?v=fko8JuUAqHM.

xviii **Much of his $400,000 salary**: MikeMcIntire and Walt Bogdanich, "At Florida State, Football Clouds Justice," *New York Times,* October 10, 2014.

xviii **Even Dr. Barron's performance goals**: "Performance Assessment of the President: The Florida State University, October 2012," FSU Board of Trustees.

xviii **largest continuous brick structure**: "Doak Campbell Stadium," *Stadiafile,* https://stadiafile.com/2012/08/31/7-doak-campbell-stadium/.

xviii **as much as $10 million**: Brian Hickey, "My View: Sports Tourism is a Team Effort," *Tallahassee Democrat,* July 11, 2015.

CHAMPIONS WAY

1 **"colloseum, religious and fortress elements"**: "Doak Campbell Stadium," *Stadiafile,* https://stadiafile.com/2012/08/31/7-doak-campbell-stadium/.

2 **earning a bachelor's degree in psychology**: Christina Lynn Suggs, curriculum vitae, 2013.

3 **Once, she filed for bankruptcy**: Petitioner Christina Suggs, Case No. 96-10349, U.S. Bankruptcy Court, District of Alabama.

3 **multiple online teaching jobs**: State of Florida v. Philbert C. Suggs, "Petition for Support and Other Relief," Case No. 14001092DR.

4 **less than $40,000**: Christina Lynn Suggs's personnel file at Florida State University.

4 **pile of student loans**: Christina Lynn Suggs's Student Aid Report for 2013–14.

4 **ran the school's distance learning program**: Mark Andrew Bonn, curriculum vitae, 2015.

5 **"Like on-ground classes"**: "Agenda for Biweekly TA Meeting," June 20, 2013.

6 **at risk of failing**: "Students That Could Fail HFT2060," spreadsheet prepared by Christie Suggs.

6 **more than a half dozen quizzes**: Christopher Casher, email message to Mark Bonn, August 1, 2013.

6 **"copied every portion"**: Aiden Sizemore, email message to Mark Bonn, July 19, 2013.

6 **"Neglect of these indications"**: "Statement on Plagiarism & Academic Fraud," Florida State University Department of History, http://history.fsu.edu/Undergraduate-Program/Statement-on-Plagiarism-Academic-Fraud

7 **senior receiver Willie Haulstead**: Bob Ferrante, "FSU receiver Willie Haulstead academically ineligible for 2013 season," *Palm Beach Post*, August 9, 2013.

7 **"Paraphrase means"**: Mark Bonn, email message to Christopher Casher, July 29, 2013.

7 **Casher then asked**: Christopher Casher, email message to Mark Bonn, August 1, 2013.

7 **"It is *unacceptable*"**: "HFT 2060: Coffee, Tea & International Culture," course syllabus, summer 2013.

7 **Casher "has legit excuses"**: Mark Bonn, email message to Christie Suggs, August 1, 2013.

7 **After linebacker Terrance Smith**: Mark Bonn, email message to Christie Suggs, July 31, 2013.

8 **He told Jernigan**: Mark Bonn, email message to Timmy Jernigan, May 5, 2013.

8 **"Brazilian coffee"**: Jarred Haggins, final project for HFT 2060, Coffee, Tea & International Culture, summer 2013, PowerPoint presentation.

8 **"take off 15 points"**: Mark Bonn, email message to Christie Suggs, August 1, 2013.

8 **"If he's enforcing"**: Aiden Sizemore, email message to Christie Suggs, August 1, 2013.

9 **"When you deal with adversity"**: Cole Harvey, "Wilder Jr. Wants to Make Most of First Full Spring," *Orlando Sentinel*, March 29, 2013.

9   **"Sorry I had to email"**: James Wilder, email message to Mark Bonn, July 25, 2013.

10 **"please use his submissions"**: Mark Bonn, email message to Christie Suggs, July 29, 2013.

10 **"at this point"**: Christie Suggs, email message to Mark Bonn, July 25, 2013.

10 **"Let me know what he asks"**: Aiden Sizemore, email message to Christie Suggs, July 25, 2013.

11 **"Let him know what he needs"**: Mark Bonn, email message to Christie Suggs, July 25, 2013.

11 **created by a tutor**: James Wilder Jr., final project for HFT 2060, Coffee, Tea & International Culture, summer 2013, PowerPoint presentation.

11 **"I am not offering"**: Christie Suggs, email message to Aiden Sizemore, July 26, 2013.

11 **"This is above both of our pay grades"**: Aiden Sizemore, email message to Christie Suggs, July 26, 2013.

11 **"Have you heard anything"**: Christie Suggs, email message to Aiden Sizemore, July 26, 2013.

12 **"Go ahead with what Dr. Bonn"**: Aiden Sizemore, email message to Christie Suggs, July 26, 2013.

NO. 34

15 **Five days before Christmas**: State of Florida vs. Michael Gibson, State Supreme Court Case No. 87530.

15 **"So, John's not home?"**: Patrick Sauer, "I Was Shot and Raped by an FSU Player," *Deadspin*, April 17, 2014, https://deadspin.com/i-was-shot-and-raped-by-an-fsu-player-i-still-cheer-fo-1563858521.

16 **The Simses were devout Baptists**: "The Sims," The W.A.Y. Ministries Inc., http://www.winningamericasyouth.org/the-sims/#our-story-1-1.

17 **the God-fearing Bowden**: Bobby Bowden and Steve Bowden, *The Wisdom of Faith* (Nashville: B&H Publishing, 2014).

17 **coveted athletic scholarship**: "Gibson: Life," WCTV, October 8, 2003, http://www.wctv.tv/home/headlines/497362.html.

17 **police later told Ashley**: Ashley Witherspoon, interview with author.

18 **"It's not uncommon"**: "2008 Football Forum: College Football Today and Tomorrow," Football Writers Association of America, http://www.sportswriters.net/fwaa/forum/2008/forum080515.

18 **When the police later interviewed Gibson**: State of Florida vs. Michael Gibson, State Supreme Court Case No. 87530.

18   **Meggs, whom everyone knew as Willie**: John C. Van Gieson, "The Lawman," *Orlando Sentinel,* September 8, 1991.

19   **"I knew his reputation"**: William Meggs, interview with author.

19   **"Willie really was my hero"**: Ashley Witherspoon, interview with author.

20   **He first joined the Seminoles**: "Bobby Bowden Bio," Florida State Seminoles Official Athletic Site, http://www.seminoles.com/View Article.dbml?ATCLID=209587899.

20   **it didn't resurface again**: "A Brief History of Florida State Football . . . ," Florida State Seminoles Media & University Information, http://www.seminoles.com/fls/32900/old_site/pdf/m-footbl/69.pdf.

20   **the first two black players**: Mark Schlabach, "Teammates Work to Restore Patterson's Place in History," ESPN, February 15, 2008, http://www.espn.com/espn/blackhistory2008/news/story?id=3246138.

21   **"Imagine what they'll say"**: Edwin Pope, "National Title Now 'Obsesses' Unique Bowden," *Miami Herald,* December 28, 1993.

22   **"She told me"**: Associated Press, "Florida coach Steve Spurrier says FSU stands for Free Shoes University," June 9, 1994.

22   **Scott Bentley was charged**: Liz Robbins, "Bentley Plea on Sex Tape: No Contest," *St. Petersburg Times,* May 17, 1994.

22   **another Florida State player, Kamari Charlton**: Alan Schmadtke, "Seminole Charged With Rape," *Orlando Sentinel,* May 18, 1994.

22   **"This," he said, "should serve"**: Christine Brennan, " 'Rough' Ride for Bowden, FSU," *Washington Post,* May 19, 1994.

23   **arrested again a few years later**: Matt Murschel, "Former Florida State Player Who Faces Caning Had Legal Woes at FSU," *Orlando Sentinel,* October 22, 2010.

23   **"That's one of the prices"**: Amy Shipley, " 'It's Embarrassing': As Florida State Wins, Image Takes a Beating," *Washington Post,* November 13, 1999.

JUST ONE MORE

25   **Z.K. was excited**: Freeh Sporkin & Sullivan LLP, *Report of the Special Investigative Counsel Regarding the Actions of the Pennsylvania State University Related to the Child Sexual Abuse Committed by Gerald A. Sandusky,* July 12, 2012, http://health-equity.pitt.edu/3956/.

26   **"And that's the last thing I remember"**: Z.K.'s testimony in Commonwealth of Pennsylvania vs. Gerald A. Sandusky, given June 14, 2012.

26   **"football runs this university"**: Freeh Sporkin & Sullivan report.

27   **$1.6 million payout**: Brian Schmitz, "Blockbuster's Premier Is a Smashing Success," *Orlando Sentinel,* December 29, 1990.

27 **"It's Paterno and Bowden"**: Tim Brant, Blockbuster Bowl telecast, Raycom Sports, December 28, 1990.

27 **On a Saturday morning**: Freeh Sporkin & Sullivan report.

28 **went to church**: Ira Josephs, "Ex-college Football Prospects Recall Making the Big Choice," *Philadelphia Inquirer,* February 5, 2001.

29 **The Sims family had tried**: "The Sims," The W.A.Y. Ministries Inc., http://www.winningamericasyouth.org/the-sims/#our-story-1-1.

29 **"We tried to help Mike"**: Kevin Record, "Head of the Class: Sims May Have Outside Chance at Starting Lineup," *News-Journal* (Daytona Beach, FL), February 8, 2003.

29 **used the family computer**: Mark Schlabach, "A Special Number: Nation's Top Prospect Can Have His Pick of Schools—and Jerseys," *Atlanta Journal-Constitution,* January 29, 2003.

30 **Bowden had a financial incentive**: Employment Agreement of Robert C. Bowden, October 1, 1999, amended November 1, 2001 and August 1, 2003.

30 **Bowden made his pilgrimage**: Christopher Lawlor, "Fla. State Has Sims' Number and He Couldn't Be Happier," *USA Today*, February 6, 2003.

31 **still faced the uphill battle**: Brent Kallestad, "Former FSU Player Again Gets Life for Rape, Shooting," Associated Press, October 7, 2003.

32 **"May God direct you"**: Bobby Bowden, letter to Judge Kathleen Dekker, August 13, 2003.

32 **"To have to come back"**: Ashley Witherspoon, interview with author.

32 **"rookie of the week"**: Josh Robbins, "'Noles Know BCS 'Love' Is Fleeting," *Orlando Sentinel,* October 28, 2003.

32 **Bobby Bowden Field**: Jeff Snook, "Bowden Wants to Wait for Recognition," *News-Journal* (Daytona Beach, FL), November 8, 2003.

APOLLO 13

33 **"What in the world"**: Brenda Monk, testimony before Committee on Infractions of the National Collegiate Athletic Association, Case No. M286, October 18, 2008.

33 **Dr. Monk was the assistant director**: ibid.

34 **"greatly enhances"**: "The Football Academic Support Staff," *2006 Florida State Football Media Guide*, ed. Jeff Purinton (Tallahassee, FL: Florida State University, 2006).

34 **$1.5-million-a-year**: Tom Farrey, "Seminoles Helped by 'LD' Diag-

noses," ESPN, December 18, 2009, http://www.espn.com/espn/otl/
news/story?id=4737281.

34 **moved to new offices**: "Athletic Academic Support Program," *2006
Florida State Football Me*dia Guide.

34 **Dr. Monk estimated**: Brenda Monk, testimony before Committee on
Infractions.

34 **"I did seek counsel"**: ibid.

35 **"If they were unable"**: ibid.

35 **"Sometimes," . . . "they would hand me"**: ibid.

35 **Al Thornton, a star**: Taylor Branch, "The Shame of College Sports,"
Atlantic Monthly, October 2011.

35 **sixty-one athletes**: Transcript of proceedings, Committee on Infractions of the National Collegiate Athletic Association, Case No. M286,
October 18, 2008.

36 **seventh serious NCAA infraction**: NCAA, *Florida State University
Public Infractions Report,* March 6, 2009. A copy can be found online
at http://assets.sbnation.com/assets/80240/FSUNCAAReport.pdf.

36 **"I kind of reflect back to *Apollo 13*"**: T. K. Wetherell, testimony before
Committee on Infractions of the National Collegiate Athletic Association, Case No. M286, October 18, 2008.

36 **"offices, conference rooms"**: "FedEx Student-Athlete Academic
Support Center," Ole Miss Rebels Official Athletic Site, http://www
.olemisssports.com/facilities/ole-facilities-academic-support-center
.html.

37 **"quiet study areas"**: "Make the Grade: Ole Miss Student-Athletes
Strive for Academic Success," University of Mississippi Foundation
News, https://umfoundation.com/home/news.php?id=460.

37 **"has kept Jeff"**: ibid.

37 **who comprise 78 percent**: Shaun R. Harper, Collin D. Williams Jr.,
Horatio W. Blackman, *Black Male Student-Athletes and Racial Inequities
in NCAA Division I College Sports* (Philadelphia: University of Pennsylvania, Center for the Study of Race and Equity in Education, 2013).

37 **cut from the team**: Coley Harvey, "Bengals Waive RB Jeff Scott,"
ESPN, June 18, 2014, http://www.espn.com/blog/cincinnati-bengals/
post/_/id/8670/bengals-jeff-scott-release-waived-running-back.

37 **giving out iPads**: "Athletics Works with University Digital First Initia-
tive," The Ohio State University Official Athletic Site, May 23, 2012,
http://www.ohiostatebuckeyes.com/genrel/052312aab.html.

37 **Jones was suspended**: Mike Hoag, "Ohio State Suspends QB Cardale Jones for Tweeting Classes Are Pointless," *Bleacher Report,* Octo-

ber 6, 2012, http://bleacherreport.com/articles/1361344-ohio-state -suspends-qb-cardale-jones-for-tweeting-classes-are-pointless.

38 **Academic Enhancement Fund**: NCAA, *2013-14 Division I Revenue Distribution Plan,* https://www.ncaa.org/sites/default/files/2013-14 Revenue Distribution Plan.pdf.

38 **about $500 million in Division I**: ibid.

38 **official four-year graduation rate**: Jake New, "More Athletes Get to Finish Line," *Inside Higher Ed,* October 29, 2014, https://www .insidehighered.com/news/2014/10/29/graduation-rates-athletes-hit -record-high.

38 **little more than a third**: University of Pennsylvania Center for the Study of Race & Equity in Education, "Black Male Student Athletes and the 2014 BCS Championship Series" (infographic), December 9, 2013, http://www.gse.upenn.edu/equity/bcs.

39 **At Antioch High School**: Michael McAdoo vs. University of North Carolina at Chapel Hill, Case No. 14-cv-935, U.S. District Court for the Middle District of North Carolina.

39 **"tall lean kid"**: "Football Recruiting—Michael McAdoo—Player Pro-files—ESPN," *RecruitingNation,* http://insider.espn.com/college-sports/ football/recruiting/player/evaluation/_/id/52531/michael-mcadoo.

39 **"My top five"**: "Mike McAdoo, Antioch" (interview with Tennessean .com), posted November 14, 2007, https://www.youtube.com/watch ?v=ynft8xqsChA.

39 **aggressively pursued him**: McAdoo vs. University of North Carolina at Chapel Hill.

39 **"I can't guarantee"**: ibid.

40 **McAdoo was steered**: ibid.

40 **for eighteen years**: Kenneth L. Wainstein, *Investigation of Irregular Classes in the Department of African and Afro-American Studies at the University of North Carolina at Chapel Hill* (Cadwalader, Wickersham & Taft LLP, 2014).

40 **"saw the paper classes"**: ibid.

41 **"and keep them eligible"**: Doris Betts et al., Report of the Ad Hoc Committee on Athletics and the University, submitted to University of North Carolina Faculty Council, December 15, 1989.

41 **"overwhelmed by an abundance"**: ibid.

41 **Times Higher Education World University Rankings**: "World Reputation Rankings 2011," Times Higher Education, https://www.times highereducation.com/world-university-rankings/2011/reputation -ranking and "World Reputation Rankings 2015," Times Higher

Education, https://www.timeshighereducation.com/world-university -rankings/2015/reputation-ranking.

41 **impermissible help**: Andy Staples, "Plagiarism Discovery Complicates McAdoo's Case Against UNC, NCAA," *Sports Illustrated*, July 8, 2011.

41 **He was picked up**: McAdoo vs. University of North Carolina at Chapel Hill.

42 **"I was sort of starstruck"**: Kadence Otto, interview with author.

43 **contract included extra bonuses**: Employment Agreement of John J. Fisher Jr., December 31, 2013.

43 **millions being spent**: Matthew R. Huml, Meg G. Hancock, Matthew J. Bergman, "Additional Support or Extravagant Cost? Student-Athletes' Perceptions on Athletic Academic Centers," *Journal of Issues in Intercollegiate Athletics* 7 (2014): 410.

44 **"We're increasingly flummoxed"**: Adam Weinstein, "Jameis Winston Isn't the Only Problem Here: An FSU Teacher's Lament," *Deadspin*, November 21, 2013, http://deadspin.com/jameis-winston-isnt-the -only-problem-here-an-fsu-teac-1467707410.

44 **the story of "Lacy"**: ibid.

SECOND CHANCES

45 **stature of his office**: Mike Strom, "Pittman May be Looking at Jail Time Today," *Times-Picayune* (New Orleans), November 18, 1998.

45 **Bowden also took up his pen**: Associated Press, "Sports News," July 17, 1987.

45 **prison for six months**: ibid.

45 **Bowden's support extended**: Alan Schmadtke, "FSU Upset That Judge Flaunted Note," *Orlando Sentinel*, May 9, 1998.

46 **Bowden claimed his letter**: ibid.

46 **"I did not understand"**: Josh Robbins, "Bowden Says His Remarks on Colorado Misconstrued," *Orlando Sentinel*, March 3, 2004.

46 **"I knew there were thousands of lost boys"**: Bobby Bowden and Mark Schlabach, *Called to Coach: Reflections on Life, Faith and Football* (New York: Simon & Schuster, 2010).

47 **Darnell Dockett, a troubled kid**: ibid.

47 **he avoided jail time**: Ray Glier, "Combustible Florida State Has Started Its Climb Back," *New York Times*, September 20, 2003.

47 **Bowden's quarterback, Adrian McPherson**: David Fleming, "Game of Chance," ESPN, March 28, 2005, http://www.espn.com/espnmag/ story?id=3760264.

47   **"I don't have any questions"**: Alan Schmadtke, "FSU Scores Small Win with List of Witnesses," *Orlando Sentinel,* June 6, 2003.

47   **another of Bowden's players**: Josh Robbins, "FSU Player Quickly Wins Acquittal on Sex Charges," *Orlando Sentinel,* August 15, 2003.

47   **skipping a final exam**: Frank Litsky, "Seminoles' Quarterback Is Ineligible for Bowl," *New York Times,* December 18, 2002.

47   **"That's an obvious question"**: Brian Landman, "Dockett Arrested on Grand Theft Charges," *St. Petersburg Times,* January 9, 2003.

48   **"Until FSU starts taking"**: Mike Bianchi, "Bowden Sends Wrong Signals on Subject of Rape," *Orlando Sentinel,* March 5, 2004.

48   **"I have known Coach Bowden"**: ibid.

48   **"Now, we understand"**: Andrew Carter, "T.K. Wetherell Goes Off the Script," *Orlando Sentinel,* March 17, 2009.

49   **had to apologize**: Brian Landman, "Florida State President T.K. Wetherell Apologizes for Obscene Remark About Samford," *Tampa Bay Times,* March 19, 2009.

50   **Paterno had 383 wins**: willy22, "How Much Will Joepa's Lead on Bowden Grow?" *Nittany Lines,* March 6, 2009, http://blogs.mcall .com/nittany_lines/2009/03/how-much-will-joepas-lead-on-bowden -grow.html

50   **"Will I ever catch him?"**: Jon Solomon, "Bobby Has Date to 'A Day With the Bowdens' Depart FSU," *Birmingham News,* July 15, 2009.

50   **"I thought to myself"**: Bobby Bowden and Mark Schlabach, *Called to Coach: Reflections on Life, Faith and Football* (New York: Simon & Schuster, 2010).

50   **pay Fisher $5 million**: Corey Clark and Jim Lamar, "Report: Bowden Expected to Retire as FSU Coach," *Tallahassee Democrat,* November 30, 2009.

50   **The end came when Wetherell**: Bowden and Schlabach, *Called to Coach.*

51   **"Joe Paterno, Educator of Men"**: Mark Wogenrich, "2011 No. 1 Regional Story: The Penn State Scandal," *Morning Call* (Allentown, PA), December 29, 2011.

51   **Sandusky at the Nittany Lion Club**: Freeh Sporkin and Sullivan LLP, *Report of the Special Investigative Counsel Regarding the Actions of The Pennsylvania State University Related to the Child Sexual Abuse Committed by Gerald A. Sandusky,* July 12, 2012, http://health-equity.pitt.edu/3956/.

52   **"If this is true"**: Cindy Boren, "Joe Paterno on Sandusky Charges," *Washington Post,* November 6, 2011.

52   **Shaken, Paterno hung up**: Pete Thamel and Mark Viera, "Penn

State's Trustees Recount Painful Decision to Fire Paterno," *New York Times,* January 18, 2012.

52 **broke down and sobbed**: Joe Posnanski, *Paterno* (New York: Simon & Schuster, 2013).

52 **the NCAA's decision**: Associated Press, "Penn State Sanctions: $60M, Bowl Ban," July 24, 2012.

52 **"I didn't want it to happen"**: Associated Press, "Bowden Gets Record in Unwelcome Way," July 24, 2012.

52 **an outpouring of testimonials**: Steve Ellis and Bill Vilona, *Pure Gold: Bobby Bowden* (Champaign, IL: Sports Publishing, 2006).

FAMOUS JAMEIS

55 **Framed news clippings**: Rachel Axon, "Dad: Family, Florida State Failed Jameis Winston," *USA Today,* May 12, 2014.

55 **brief cell phone video**: Jameis Winston, Instagram post, posted June 2014, https://www.instagram.com/jaboowins5.

57 **"Hey, college football is tough"**: Mike Tankersley, "Fisher: FSU Back Where It Belongs," *Montgomery Advertiser,* February 8, 2012.

57 **"Honestly," . . . "money is probably the biggest factor"**: Brandon Parker, "Famous Jameis," ESPN, May 15, 2012, http://www.espn .com/high-school/football/story/_/id/7919785/two-sport-phenom -jameis-winston-bright-future-football-baseball.

58 **caught stealing crab legs**: Alina Machado and Mariano Castillo, "FSU's Jameis Winston Accused of Stealing Crab Legs," CNN, May 1, 2014, http://www.cnn.com/2014/04/30/us/florida-winston-shop lifting-allegation/.

58 **stop taking soda**: "'He's Stealing Soda' Burger King Employee Told Cops in 2013 Call," TMZ, May 21, 2014, http://www.tmz.com/ 2014/05/21/jameis-winston-stealing-soda-burger-king-employee -stealing-soda-911/.

58 **crude Internet meme**: Jessica Glenza, "Jameis Winston Suspended for Whole Game as FSU Extends Quarterback's Ban," *Guardian*, September 20, 2014.

58 **"I think it would show"**: Axon, "Dad: Family, Florida State."

58 **Winston got to know a medical student**: Confidential source, interview by author.

58 **would lead her to seek counseling**: Deposition of Melissa Ashton, Erica Kinsman v. Florida State University Board of Trustees, Case No. 6:15-cv-00235, June 24, 2015.

58 **"was of such a nature"**: Walt Bogdanich, "A Star Player Accused, and a Flawed Rape Investigation," *New York Times*, April 16, 2014.

59 **fifty or more sexual partners:** Confidential source, interview by author.

59 **"it's kind of a football player thing"**: Chris Casher, recorded interview with Tallahassee Police Department, Case No. 12-32758, November 14, 2013.

59 **stopped at gunpoint**: Florida State University Police Case No. 1211-0248, November 25, 2012.

59 **Winston and Casher returned**: Tallahassee Police Department Case No. 12-031814, November 27, 2012.

61 **yet another incident**: Tallahassee Police Department Case No. 12-029851, November 4, 2012.

61 **"Purgatory Thursday"**: Report of Investigator Jason Newlin, Office of the State Attorney, Leon County, on Jameis Winston case, December 5, 2013.

62 **"I mean, like, if you want to"**: ibid.

62 **"meet me out front"**: ibid.

62 **"Should I go?"**: ibid.

62 **thought she seemed drunk**: Confidential source, interview by author.

62 **Description of cab ride**: Report of Investigator Jason Newlin, Office of the State Attorney, Leon County, on Jameis Winston case, December 5, 2013.

62 **forcing himself on her**: ibid.

63 **"Dude," . . . "she's telling you to stop"**: Erica Kinsman v. Jameis Winston, Case No. 6:15-cv-00696, U.S. District Court for the Middle District of Florida.

63 **"You crazy"**: Complainant's Post-Hearing Memorandum, Florida State University Investigative Hearing in the Matter of Erica Kinsman and Jameis Winston, May 8, 2015.

63 **pushing her face to the tile**: *The Hunting Ground,* directed by Kirby Dick (Los Angeles: Chain Camera Pictures/The Weinstein Company, 2015).

63 **"Okay," . . . "you can leave now"**: ibid.

63 **would not face her**: Report of Investigator Jason Newlin.

63 **"come find me," "please call me"**: ibid.

64 **One of those friends**: ibid.

64 **"vaginal tenderness"**: Tallahassee Police Department Case No. 12-32758, December 7, 2012.

64 **crawled into her hospital bed**: Complainant's Post-Hearing Memorandum.

65 **thought he looked concerned**: Report of Investigator Jason Newlin.

65 **The police had been doing little**: ibid.

65 **He sent an email**: Scott Angulo, email message to Sergeants Baldwin and Johnson, January 11, 2013.

65 **"This is a huge football town"**: *The Hunting Ground,* directed by Kirby Dick (Los Angeles: Chain Camera Pictures/The Weinstein Company, 2015).

65 **called him on his cell phone**: Tallahassee Police Department Case No. 12-32758, December 7, 2012.

66 **Phone records show**: Kinsman v. FSU Board of Trustees.

66 **case was effectively shelved**: Walt Bogdanich, "A Star Player Accused, and a Flawed Rape Investigation," *New York Times,* April 16, 2014.

66 **Asked later why he had not told anyone**: Deposition of John Fisher, Kinsman v. FSU Board of Trustees, given on September 22, 2015.

66 **He played in his first**: Corey Clark, "Fisher Stresses Patience for QB Spot," *Tallahassee Democrat,* April 15, 2013.

67 **"But the guy's gonna stumble"**: Ira Schoffel, "Full Speed Ahead for FSU's Winston," *Tallahassee Democrat,* May 15, 2013.

INSANITY

71 **embodiment of a Southern gentleman**: William E. King, *If Gargoyles Could Talk: Sketches of Duke University* (Durham, NC: Carolina Academic Press, 1997).

71 **"had little to say"**: ibid.

71 **"the greatest man"**: Robert H. Woody, *Dictionary of North Carolina Biography* (Durham, NC: University of North Carolina Press, 1986).

72 **At least eighteen players died**: "Deaths From Football Playing," *Washington Post,* October 15, 1905.

72 **"I believe in outdoor games"**: "Hears Football Men," *Washington Post,* October 10, 1905.

73 **founding football coach**: King, *If Gargoyles Could Talk.*

73 **The first football coach**: Ric A. Kabat, "Before the Seminoles: Football at Florida State College, 1902–1904," *Florida Historical Quarterly* 78, no. 1 (July 1991): 20.

73 **"debating societies are more beneficial"**: ibid.

73 **"arm chair football critic"**: J.A. Forsythe, "The Game of Foot-Ball," *The University News* (Gainesville, FL), October 19, 1906.

74 **"To a young and growing university"**: ibid.

74 **"exaggerated emphasis"**: William P. Few, "The Excessive Devotion to Athletics," *The South Atlantic Quarterly* 5, no. 1 (January 1906).

76 **"Sanity Code"**: Andrew Zimbalist, *Unpaid Professionals: Commercialism*

and Conflict in Big-Time College Sports (Princeton, NJ: Princeton University Press, 1999).

76 **"The restrictions in the Sanity Code"**: Christopher J. Walsh, *Where Football is King: A History of the SEC* (Lanham, MD: Taylor Trade Publishing, 2006).

76 **referred to as "student-athletes"**: Robert A. McCormick and Amy Christian McCormick, "The Myth of the Student-Athlete: The College Athlete as Employee," *Washington Law Review* 81 (2006):71.

77 **"In fact," . . . "the state conducted institution"**: Walter Byers and Charles H. Hammer, *Unsportsmanlike Conduct: Exploiting College Athletes* (Ann Arbor, MI: University of Michigan Press, 1995).

77 **C.F. Mueller Company**: Harvey P. Dale, "About the UBIT," chap. 9 in *New York University Eighteenth Conference on Tax Planning for 501(c)(3) Organizations* (New York: Matthew Bender, 1990).

78 **"athletic activities of schools"**: Scott R. Rosner and Kenneth L. Shropshire, *The Business of Sports* (Sudbury, MA: Jones and Bartlett, 2004).

78 **"related to the education function"**: Sheldon Cohen, interview with author.

79 **It took root in Bristol**: David Bauder, "ESPN Turns 20," Associated Press, September 5, 1999.

79 **"And we're just minutes away"**: Mancini ESPN, "1979—ESPN, commercials—First Day/3 months: SportsCenter, NCAA," recorded on September 7, 1979, posted on March 15, 2015, https://www.youtube.com/watch?v=v0ed1dkqHZY.

79 **paid $305,000**: Mark Asher, "Hoyas-Terps 'Iffy' for Next Year," *Washington Post*, March 15, 1980.

79 **would offer $100 million**: Brett McMurphy and Andy Katz, "Report: $100 Million for Football Schools," ESPN, March 5, 2013, http://www.espn.com/espnw/news-commentary/article/9019093/big-east-football-schools-keep-close-110-million-league-split-according-report.

80 **worth $5.6 billion**: Rachel Bachman, "ESPN Strikes Deal for College Football Playoff," *Wall Street Journal*, November 21, 2012.

80 **"Their reasoning was probably wrong"**: Richard Schmalbeck, interview with author.

80 **total of $8 billion**: Paula Lavigne, "College Sports Thrive Amid Downturn," ESPN, May 1, 2014, http://www.espn.com/espn/otl/story/_/id/10851446/sports-programs-nation-top-public-colleges-thrived-economic-downturn-earning-record-revenues.

81 **generated $50 million**: "NCAA Finances," *USA Today*, http://sports.usatoday.com/ncaa/finances/.

81 **Seminole IMG College**: "Florida State University: IMG College Client Since 2007," IMG College: America's Home for College Sports, http://www.imgcollege.com/our-properties/colleges-universities/florida-state-university.

81 **"the nation's top collegiate properties"**: IMG College: America's Home for College Sports, http://www.imgcollege.com/.

81 **"It's sort of a fraud"**: John Colombo, interview with author.

82 **left his razor at home**: Andrew Greif, "Oregon Ducks' Secondary Violations Include Shaving Supplies, Laser Tag and Mini Golf," *Oregonian* (Portland, OR), August 5, 2014.

82 **In an internal memo**: Confidential Report to the Executive Committee Administrative Subcommittee, August 1, 2007, to July 31, 2008.

83 **"Games are festooned"**: Keller v. Electronic Arts, Inc., Case No. 4:09-cv-1967, U.S. District Court, Northern District of California.

83 **"I went to UConn"**: Deposition of Tate George in Oscar P. Robertson, Tate George and Ray Ellis vs. NCAA et al, Case No. 11-cv-00388, U.S. District Court, Northern District of California, March 9, 2012.

84 **Renfro groped for solutions**: Wally I. Renfro, email message to Mark Emmert, October 17, 2010.

BIGNESS AND PROSPERITY

85 **about $20 million**: Alan Schmadtke, "FSU Athletic Board Approves Largest Budget in School History," *Orlando Sentinel,* June 3, 1993.

85 **to $90 million**: "NCAA Finances," *USA Today,* http://sports.usatoday.com/ncaa/finances/.

85 **$80 million in improvements**: Jennifer Portman, "FSU Trustees OK Bond Sale for Doak Campbell Upgrades," *Tallahassee Democrat,* March 6, 2015.

85 **reflected in its checkbook**: Knight Commission on Intercollegiate Athletics, "Athletics U Academic Spending Database for NCAA Division I," http://spendingdatabase.knightcommission.org/.

86 **Among the trustees present**: Florida State University, "Board of Trustees," https://trustees.fsu.edu/trustees/.

86 **Downtown Getdown**: Robert Wood Johnson Foundation, "Anheuser-Busch and the #1 Party School," March 23, 2009, http://www.rwjf.org/en/library/articles-and-news/2009/03/anheuser-busch-and-the-1-party-school.html.

87 **When it came time to discuss**: "FSU Board of Trustees Meeting,

June 7, 2013," Florida State University Board of Trustees, http://
learningforlife.capd.fsu.edu/bot/jun7_13.htm.

89 **"Right from the beginning"**: Ned Stuckey-French, interview with
author.

89 **mission statement**: Florida State University, "About Florida State,"
https://www.fsu.edu/about/mission_vision.html.

90 **auctioned them off for $105,000**: Zac Ellis, "Alabama's Broken 2011
BCS Trophy Sells at Auction for $105K," *Sports Illustrated,* May 20,
2013.

90 **Only 20 of the 128 schools**: *Revenues and Expenses: NCAA Division
I Intercollegiate Athletics Programs Report, 2004–2013* (Indianapolis:
National Collegiate Athletic Association, 2014), http://www.ncaa
publications.com/productdownloads/D1REVEXP2013.pdf.

91 **"It's hard to link them"**: Ben Jones, "BCS Title Affects FSU University as a Whole," *Warchant,* April 16, 2014, https://floridastate.rivals
.com/news/bcs-title-affects-fsu-university-as-a-whole.

91 **"There's nothing that stood out"**: ibid.

91 **Outside the top tier**: *Revenues and Expenses: NCAA Division I Intercollegiate Athletics Progra*ms Report.

91 **none of the 280 teams**: Joint Legislative Audit and Review Commis-
sion, *Review of Non-Academic Services and Costs at Virginia's Public Higher
Education Institutions: Report to the Governor and the General Assembly of
Virginia* (Richmond, VA: September 2013).

92 **plow the $10 million**: Ty West, "UAB Dropping Football, Cites Costs
and Changing NCAA Landscape," *Birmingham Business Journal,*
December 2, 2014.

92 **an angry mob**: Ry Rivard, "Sacking Football in Alabama," *Inside High-
erEd,* December 3, 2014, https://www.insidehighered.com/news/
2014/12/03/u-alabama-birmingham-sacks-its-football-team-citing
-costs.

92 **"vehicle to get us to greatness"**: Jon Solomon, "UAB Football is Back,
Questions Remain," CBS Sports, June 1, 2015, http://www.cbssports
.com/college-football/news/uab-football-is-back-reinstatement
-announcement-set-for-monday/.

93 **"My guess is we need to be looking"**: David M. Hale, "Florida State
Hires Stan Wilcox," ESPN, August 7, 2013, http://www.espn.com/
college-sports/story/_/id/9548157/florida-state-seminoles-hire-stan
-wilcox-ad.

UNCLE LUKE

94 **beloved aunt, Tamekia Brown**: Vaughn McClure, "New Number Meaningful to Freeman," ESPN, September 5, 2014, http://www.espn.com/blog/nfcsouth/post/_/id/56751/new-number-meaningful-to-freeman.

94 **man of the house**: Natalie Pierre, "Football Helped FSU's Devonta Freeman Escape Tough Background," *Tallahassee Democrat*, May 13, 2014.

94 **"She meant so much"**: McClure, "New Number Meaningful to Freeman."

95 **$300 of his financial aid**: Luther Campbell, "Devonta Freeman Will Be an NFL Star," *Miami New Times*, May 1, 2014.

95 **cousin had been shot dead**: Coley Harvey, "One Month After Cousin's Death, FSU RB Devonta Freeman Returns Home to Miami," *Orlando Sentinel*, October 21, 2012.

95 **At $50 per funeral**: Manny Navarro, "Devonta Freeman Reflects on Tough Miami Upbringing as NFL Draft Approaches," *Miami Herald*, May 7, 2014.

96 **"Devonta Freeman was one of the nicest"**: Luther Campbell, *The Book of Luke: My Fight for Truth, Justice & Liberty City* (New York: Harper Collins, 2015).

96 **"Their dedication and concentration"**: ibid.

96 **"a second father"**: Timothy Bella, "Devonta Freeman Sets Sights on NFL, Lifting Others Out of Miami's Projects," *AlJazeera America*, May 9, 2014, http://america.aljazeera.com/articles/2014/5/9/devonta-freeman-draft.html.

96 **"He was like, 'Man, you're going to have to grow up'"**: Devonta Freeman, *The Jim Rome Show*, CBS Sports Radio, November 4, 2013, http://jimrome.com/2016/01/05/devonta-freeman/.

97 **"I was warning him"**: Luther Campbell, "Why I Stick Around," *Miami New Times*, February 11, 2016.

97 **a platinum-haired woman**: Luke Enterprise web site, www.luke-enterprise.com (cached September 24, 2005).

97 **he was involved with youth football**: Liberty City Optimist Club of Florida Inc., 2005 annual report.

98 **pursued for child support**: Jennifer Lebovich, "Luther Campbell Free After Arrest in Paternity Case," *Miami Herald*, February 19, 2009.

98 **five women**: Greg Bishop, "Former Hip-Hop Artist's Defense Never Rests," *New York Times*, November 5, 2012.

98   **serving as defensive coordinator**: Matt Porter, "Luther Campbell Joins Miami Norland Coaching Staff," *Palm Beach Post,* January 30, 2014.

98   **"to maintain good moral character"**: Luther Roderick Campbell v. Commissioner of Education, Case No. 11-0124-D, Education Practices Commission of the State of Florida.

98   **"produced and published"**: ibid.

98   **string of criminal charges**: ibid.

99   **"aiding or procuring"**: ibid.

99   **dispute over legal fees**: "Campbell Slams Child Custody Reports," WENN Entertainment News Wire Service, February 21, 2009.

99   **"entertainment efforts"**: Campbell v. Commissioner of Education.

99   **"Impressionable inner-city youth"**: ibid.

100 **"got kids off the dangerous streets"**: ibid.

100 **"has decided to help"**: ibid.

100 **"Unclelukesworld"**: Uncle Luke's World web site, http://www.uncle lukesworld.com (cached February 11, 2003).

100 **"xxxluke.com"**: Uncle Luke's XXX Peep Show, http://www.xxxluke .com (cached March 8, 2005).

101 **"Campbell intends to go further"**: ibid.

101 **A detailed, twenty-one-page business plan**: "Luke Enterprises Business Plan," Exhibit 1-C, Aueishua Buckner v. Luther Campbell, Case No. 09-22815, U.S. District Court, Southern District of Florida.

101 **"The old adage 'sex sells'"**: ibid.

101 **Luke Sports & Entertainment**: Articles of Incorporation for Luke Sports & Entertainment Inc., March 15, 2006.

101 **Allen and Campbell briefly explored**: Deposition of Sean Allen, In Re: Capitol Investments USA, Inc. and Nevin Karey Shapiro, Case No. 09-36408, U.S. Bankruptcy Court, Southern District of Florida, December 19, 2011.

101 **Shapiro was a crook**: Jonathan Stempel, "Architect of $930 Million Ponzi Scheme Gets 20 Year Term," Reuters, June 7, 2011, http://www .reuters.com/article/us-ponzi-shapiro-sentencing-idUSTRE7567B 520110607.

102 **Shapiro's lurid accusations**: Charles Robinson, "Renegade Miami Football Booster Spells Out Illicit Benefits to Players," Yahoo Sports, August 16, 2011, http://sports.yahoo.com/news/renegade-miami -football-booster-spells-213700753--spt.html.

102 **Allen peppered Freeman**: Jay Weaver and Manny Navarro, "Testimony of Sean 'Pee Wee' Allen Could Bring Miami Hurricanes Program to its Knees," *Miami Herald,* October 7, 2012.

102 **"I had never asked a player"**: ibid.

103 **a *Miami Herald* investigation**: Ken Rodriguez and Dan Le Batard, "Ex-Canes: We Played for Pay," *Miami Herald,* May 20, 1994.

103 **"If they don't start Ryan Collins"**: Dan Le Batard, "Campbell Threatens to 'Tell All' if Collins Isn't Named Starter," *Miami Herald,* March 31, 1995.

103 **"Luther Campbell was the first"**: Robinson, "Renegade Miami Football Booster."

103 **sued him for libel**: Luther Campbell v. Nevin Shapiro, Case No. 11-30137-CA-21, Circuit Court of the 11th Judicial Circuit, Miami-Dade County.

103 **"That punk could never be me"**: Luther Campbell, "Nevin Shapiro Can Kiss My Ass," *Miami New Times,* August 17, 2011.

103 **later dropped the suit**: Barry Jackson, "Sports Buzz," *Miami Herald,* July 23, 2016.

MORAL COMPASS

105 **When Christie Suggs sat down**: Christina Lynn Suggs Student Aid Report, 2013–14.

106 **workload rubric**: Agenda for Biweekly TA Meeting, June 20, 2013.

106 **thirty hours a week**: Shannon Buck, email message to Christie Suggs, June 19, 2013.

106 **"It was marvelous to watch her"**: Barbara Davis, interview with author.

107 **"Professor Suggs is amazing!"**: Performance evaluations of Christina Lynn Suggs, 2011.

107 **liked her efforts**: Shannon Buck, email message to Christie Suggs, May 20, 2013.

108 **rushed for 1,600 yards**: Matt Baker, "Plant Product James Wilder Jr. Leaving Florida State for NFL," *Tampa Bay Times,* January 9, 2014.

108 **"There might not be a more freakish athlete"**: "Football Recruiting— James Wilder Jr.—Player Profiles—ESPN," *RecruitingNation,* http://insider.espn.com/college-sports/football/recruiting/player/evaluation/_/id/96998/james-wilder-jr.

108 **"They said, 'We know we can sleep well'"**: Eduardo A. Encina, "Plant's Wilder Chooses Florida State," *Tampa Bay Times,* August 18, 2010.

108 **nearly eight hundred yards**: "James Wilder Jr. Bio," Florida State Seminoles Official Athletic Site, http://www.seminoles.com/ViewArticle.dbml?ATCLID=209587811.

108 **On the morning of February 22, 2012**: Leon County Sheriff's Office

Arrest/Probable Cause Affidavit for James C. Wilder, Case No. 2012CF609.

109 **"After we exited the bathroom"**: ibid.

109 **"I don't have to give you"**: ibid.

109 **charge was downgraded**: Coley Harvey, "FSU RB James Wilder Suspended After Felony Arrests," *Orlando Sentinel,* February 22, 2012.

110 **"Hopefully we can resolve this"**: ibid.

110 **Wilder was on probation**: Judgment, Case No. 2012CF609, Circuit Court, Second Judicial Circuit for Leon County, Fla.

110 **he was arrested again**: Affidavit for Violation of Probation, Case No. 2012CF609.

110 **"We're going to try and see"**: D.C. Reeves, "James Wilder Jr. Arrested for Probation Violation," *Warchant,* June 22, 2012, https://floridastate.rivals.com/news/james-wilder-jr-arrested-for-probation-violation.

110 **arrested yet again**: "Florida State's Wilder Arrested, Misses Court Appearance," *Sports Illustrated,* January 7, 2013.

110 **"Just keep moving forward"**: Jenna Laine, "James Wilder Jr. and Father Grew Closer During Early Struggles at FSU," *Sports Talk Florida,* March 18, 2014, http://www.sportstalkflorida.com/nfl/nfl-news/james-wilder-jr-and-father-grew-closer-during-early-struggles-at-fsu/.

111 **had filed for divorce**: Amended Petition for Dissolution of Marriage, Alice Englert Bonn petitioner, Mark Andrew Bonn respondent, Case No. 2012DR3248, Circuit Court, Second Judicial Circuit for Leon County, Florida.

111 **restraining order against him**: Petition for Injunction for Protection Against Domestic Violence, Dr. Mark Bonn respondent, case No. 2012DR3095, Circuit Court, Second Judicial Circuit for Leon County, Florida.

111 **divorced from his first wife**: Petition for Dissolution of Marriage, Kimberly M. Bonn vs. Mark Andrew Bonn, Case No. 1998DR002361, Circuit Court, Second Judicial Circuit for Leon County, Florida.

111 **he was charged**: State vs. Mark Andrew Bonn, Case No. 1998MM005133, Second Judicial Circuit for Leon County, Fla.

111 **where he had been since 1989**: Mark Andrew Bonn, curriculum vitae, 2015.

112 **.338 batting average**: "Mark Bonn—LinkedIn," https://www.linkedin.com/in/mark-bonn-80748214.

112 **niece of Ron Sellers**: "Florida State Alumna's Planned Gift to Support Dedman," *Dedman School of Hospitality Summer 2015 Newsletter,*

http://business.fsu.edu/docs/default-source/cob/Department-Docs/
dshnewsletter-summer2015.pdf.

112   **some featuring Bowden**: Old School Open web site, http://oldschool
open.com/photos.php.

112   **ceremonial $20,000 check**: "Celebrating Excellence," *Dedman School
of Hospitality Winter 2014 Newsletter,* http://business.fsu.edu/docs/
default-source/cob/Department-Docs/dshnewsletter-winter2014.pdf.

112   **"keep myself in good academic place"**: James Wilder, email message
to Mark Bonn, July 25, 2013.

112   **traveling in St. Louis**: Mark Bonn, email message to James Wilder,
July 25, 2013.

113   **"His average is now a 57.2%"**: Christie Suggs, email message to Mark
Bonn, July 25, 2013.

113   **till 5 p.m. Saturday**: Mark Bonn, email message to Christie Suggs,
July 26, 2013.

113   **Christie shared her concerns**: Christie Suggs, email message to
Aiden Sizemore, July 25, 2013.

113   **"unorthodox"**: Aiden Sizemore, email message to Christie Suggs,
July 25, 2013.

113   **"star running back"**: Mark Bonn, email message to Christie Suggs,
July 25, 2013.

113   **"send him an email"**: Mark Bonn, email message to Christie Suggs,
July 27, 2013.

113   **a one-line message**: James Wilder, email message to Mark Bonn, July
29, 2013.

113   **"Ok James"**: Mark Bonn, email message to James Wilder, July 29,
2013.

114   **"James," . . . "can you see me"**: Mark Bonn, email message to James
Wilder, July 29, 2013.

114   **"My grade in the class should be a B now"**: James Wilder, email message to Mark Bonn, August 1, 2013.

114   **"It looks great"**: Mark Bonn, emai message to Christie Suggs, August
1, 2013.

115   **"Please let me know when you are available"**: Carolyn Egan, email
message to Christie Suggs, August 29, 2013.

115   **"more than just the academic dishonesty"**: Email from David
Paradice to Caryn Beck-Dudley, July 31, 2013.

115   **"Clearly our discussion"**: Caryn Beck-Dudley, email message to
Karen Laughlin, August 2, 2013.

116   **Christie reached out**: Christie Suggs, email message to Sam McCall,
October 4, 2013.

116 **"I'm a little worried"**: Christie Suggs, email message to Jane Ohlin, October 6, 2013.

116 **a pay raise of one dollar an hour**: Susan Hochstein, email message to Jennifer Tobias, September 17, 2013.

116 **"You won't be losing your job"**: Jane Ohlin, email message to Christie Suggs, October 7, 2013.

116 **"They were asking her to pad grades"**: Phil Suggs, interview with author.

117 **"She had been told how there had been tremendous pressure"**: Barbara Davis, interview with author.

117 **"She was told that what she did"**: Melissa Izaak, interview with author.

SCANDAL

121 **"Dear Colleague" letter**: "Dear Colleague Letter from Assistant Secretary for Civil Rights Russlynn Ali," U.S. Department of Education, Office for Civil Rights, April 4, 2011, http://www2.ed.gov/about/offices/list/ocr/letters/colleague-201104.html.

122 **budget for athletics skyrocketed**: Jake New, "The Temptation of Baylor," *Inside Higher Ed,* November 9, 2015, https://www.insidehigher ed.com/news/2015/11/09/football-and-faith-temptation-baylor.

122 **$266 million stadium**: J.B. Smith, "Stadium Rising: The Story of McLane Stadium, from Start to Finish," *Waco Tribune,* August 29, 2014.

122 **$4 million a year**: Mark Schlabach, "How Bad was Baylor Before Briles?" ESPN, December 29, 2013, http://www.espn.com/college -football/bowls13/story/_/id/10204960/examining-just-how-bad -baylor-was-art-briles-rebuild-bears.

122 **eight thousand season-ticket holders**: Don Muret, "Baylor's Waterfront Home Keys Development," *Street & Smith's Sports Business Journal,* September 8, 2014, http://www.sportsbusinessdaily.com/Journal/ Issues/2014/09/08/Facilities/Baylor-stadium.aspx.

122 **"criminal background checks"**: "Baylor University Board of Regents Findings of Fact," Baylor University, May 2016, https://www.baylor .edu/rtsv/doc.php/266596.pdf.

122 **One of them, Sam Ukwuachu**: Jessica Luther, "Silence at Baylor," *Texas Monthly,* August 20, 2015.

122 **The other, Shawn Oakman**: Philip Ericksen, "Oakman Named in 2013 Incident Report Alleging Assault," *Waco Tribune,* April 25, 2016.

123 **Tevin Elliot was accused**: Paula Lavigne, "Baylor Faces Accusations of Ignoring Sex Assault Victims," ESPN, February 2, 2016, http://www

.espn.com/espn/otl/story/_/id/14675790/baylor-officials-accused
-failing-investigate-sexual-assaults-fully-adequately-providing-support
-alleged-victims.

123   **Briles was fired**: Mark Schlabach and Paula Lavigne, "Art Briles
Acknowledges Role in Baylor Scandal," ESPN, September 10, 2016,
http://www.espn.com/college-football/story/_/id/17510465/art-briles
-former-baylor-bears-coach-says-takes-responsibility-mishandled-sexual
-assault-allegations.

123   **"significant concerns"**: "Baylor University Board of Regents Findings
of Fact."

123   **"Baylor failed"**: ibid.

125   **"golden triangle"**: Howard L. Nixon, *The Athletic Trap* (Baltimore:
Johns Hopkins University Press, 2014).

125   **football player, Michael Dyer**: Kurt Voigt, "Police Investigate Michael
Dyer Traffic Stop," Associated Press, July 30, 2012.

126   **Denney was fired**: David Harten, "State Trooper Involved in Dyer
Stop Fired, Submits Appeal," *Arkansas Democrat-Gazette* (Little Rock,
AR), August 2, 2012.

126   **"The sheriff was a friend of the program"**: Josh Peter, "Former Oklahoma Coach Barry Switzer Admits He Covered Up Minor Charges
Against Players," *USA Today*, October 9, 2014.

126   **including Christian Peter**: Josh Peter, "Christian Peter Knows
Domestic Abuse," *USA Today*, December 16, 2014.

126   **Lawrence Phillips, who took part**: Linda Robertson, "Phillips Departs,
But the Hypocrisy in College Sports Will Stay Behind," Knight-
Ridder Newspapers, January 5, 1996.

127   **"T. K. said, 'Are you going to hurt us?'"**: Confidential source, interview with author.

127   **Travis Johnson, was accused**: Rich McKay and Josh Robbins, "FSU
Tried to Protect Player in Rape Case," *Orlando Sentinel*, August 15, 2003.

127   **"was trying to cover up"**: Bob Mahlburg and Josh Robbins, "Report:
School Handled Rape Charge Poorly," *Sun-Sentinel* (Fort Lauderdale,
FL), August 23, 2003.

127   **"bizarre, at best"**: Rich McKay and Josh Robbins, "FSU Officials
Tried to Broker Rape Deal," *Sun-Sentinel* (Fort Lauderdale, FL),
August 15, 2003.

128   **"I learned quickly"**: Walt Bogdanich, "A Star Player Accused and a
Flawed Rape Investigation," *New York Times*, April 16, 2014.

128   **"I asked what was wrong"**: Testimony of Georgia Northway in trial of
Gregory Dent, Case No. 2013CF1888, Second Judicial Circuit, Leon
County, Fla., September 24, 2014.

129   **thought of him as a brother**: Testimony of D.R., ibid.

129   **"After a couple of increasingly forceful attempts"**: Tallahassee
       Police Department Arrest/Probable Cause Affidavit for Gregory L.
       Dent, Case No. 2013CF1888.

129   **partially penetrated her**: ibid.

130   **investigator Laura Gereg**: Recorded interview, Tallahassee Police
       Department, June 9, 2013.

130   **"It's a very serious offense"**: David Hale, "WR Greg Dent Charged
       With Rape," ESPN, June 11, 2013, http://www.espn.com/ncf/story/_/
       id/9360575/greg-dent-florida-state-seminoles-facing-sexual-assault
       -charges.

131   **jailed a second time**: Leon County Sheriff's Office Arrest/Probable
       Cause Affidavit for Gregory L. Dent, Case No. 2013CF1888, January
       22, 2014.

131   **"That's the first text message"**: Nathan Prince, recording of trial of
       Gregory Dent, Case No. 2013CF1888, Second Judicial Circuit, Leon
       County, Fla., September 24, 2014.

131   **"I'm not thinking"**: Testimony of D.R., ibid.

132   **"the go sign"**: Testimony of Greg Dent, ibid.

132   **not guilty of sexual assault**: Sean Rossman, "Former FSU WR Dent
       Guilty of Misdemeanor Battery," *Tallahassee Democrat,* September 30,
       2014.

133   **"extremely happy"**: ibid.

133   **"He'll text us"**: Brendan Sonnone, "FSU Has Not Ruled Out Possi-
       bility of Greg Dent Returning to Football Team," *Orlando Sentinel,*
       September 30, 2014.

IN THE RED ZONE

134   **"face enormous risk"**: Mike McIntire and Walt Bogdanich, "At Flor-
       ida State, Football Clouds Justice," *New York Times,* October 10, 2014.

135   **twenty complaints of sexual assault**: Deposition of Melissa Ashton,
       Erica Kinsman v. Florida State University Board of Trustees, Case
       No. 6:15-cv-00235, U.S. District Court for the Middle District of Flor-
       ida, June 24, 2015.

135   **After graduating from**: ibid.

135   **"They were still distraught"**: ibid.

136   **results of her blood work**: ibid.

138   **second female student**: ibid.

138   **left after one quarter**: ibid.

138   **Matt Baker's kitchen phone rang**: Matt Baker, "Jameis Winston and

Me: The Pain of Covering the Scandal," *Tampa Bay Times*, February 26, 2015.

138   **He had landed in Tampa**: "Matt Baker—LinkedIn," https://www .linkedin.com/in/matt-baker-29803a9.

139   **"I was writing a high school sports story"**: Matt Baker, interview by author.

139   **"Can you share any details"**: David Perry, email message to Chris Connell, November 8, 2013.

139   **Chief Perry then forwarded**: David Perry, email message to Monk Bonasorte, November 9, 2013.

140   **circulating the reporter's résumé**: Eliott Finebloom, email message to Monk Bonasorte, November 9, 2013.

140   **"talk to Jimbo"**: Monk Bonasorte, email message to David Perry, November 9, 2013.

140   **obtained signed statements**: Affidavits of Ronald Darby and Christopher Casher, November 13, 2013.

140   **ninety-nine telephone calls**: Monk Bonasorte telephone records.

140   **called the Tallahassee police**: Deposition of Melissa Ashton, Kinsman v. FSU Board of Trustees.

140   **he angrily contacted**: ibid.

141   **"Jeanine said to me"**: ibid.

141   **"Thank you for contacting me"**: Jim Russell, email message to Brad Appleton, November 12, 2013.

141   **"I emailed a few days ago"**: Matt Baker, email message to Scott Beck, November 8, 2013.

141   **decided to go with it**: "Florida State QB Jameis Winston Investigated for Sexual Assault," TMZ, November 13, 2013.

142   **"preparing a defense"**: Kevin Vaughan, "Documents: Police, FSU Hampered Jameis Winston Investigation," Fox Sports, October 10, 2014, http://www.foxsports.com/college-football/story/jameis-winston-florida -state-tallahassee-police-hindered-investigation-documents-101014.

143   **Online commenters**: Declaration of Baine Kerr, Kinsman v. FSU Board of Trustees.

143   **sisters were demonized**: ibid.

143   **"That was just my experience"**: Deposition of Melissa Ashton, Kinsman v. FSU Board of Trustees.

143   **"For my role"**: Baker, "Jameis Winston and Me."

144   **gambling web site**: "Are You Guys Going to Take Duke +29 Before the Jameis Winston Decision at 2PM?" *Sports Book Review* Forum, http://www.sportsbookreview.com/forum/players-talk/2718134-you -guys-going-take-duke-29-before-jameis-winston-decison-2pm.html.

145   **gotten rid of the phone**: Rachel Axon, "Jameis Winston Doesn't Appear at Teammates' Hearing," *USA Today,* May 20, 2014.

145   **"There's only one person"**; Willie Meggs, interview with author.

146   **"she got caught up in a mess"**: ibid.

146   **"a recurring problem"**: Walt Bogdanich, "A Star Player Accused and a Flawed Rape Investigation," *New York Times,* April 16, 2014.

146   **"I belive that Mr. Winston cannot be convicted"**: ibid.

146   **"all the things I've been through"**: Associated Press, "Florida State QB Jameis Winston Wins Heisman Trophy," December 15, 2013.

TOUCHDOWN

147   **straight to the videotape**: Tallahassee Police Department Probable Cause Affidavit for Ira Lee Denson Jr., Case No. 13-33570.

147   **passing worthless checks**: State vs. Delmarick Pender, case No. 2013MM000852.

148   **$22 million apiece**: Patrick Rishe, "The Economics of Late-Season Success in College Football," *Forbes,* December 1, 2013.

149   **his half brother, Timothy Pruitt**: Tallahassee Police Department Probable Cause Affidavit for Tarron J. Addison, Case No. 13-33742.

150   **"He conceded he could have gotten out of the car"**: Tallahassee Police Department Probable Cause Affidavit for Ira Lee Denson Jr., Case No. 13-33742.

151   **issued a press release**: Tallahassee Police Department, "Police Investigating Shooting; Incident Occurred at Seminole Ridge Apartments," City of Tallahassee, December 24, 2013, http://www.talgov .com/tpd/News/Police-Investigating-Shooting-4050.aspx.

151   **"all of us wished would just go away"**: Bob Gabordi, "The Story Behind Our Jameis Winston Story," *Tallahassee Democrat,* November 14, 2013.

152   **"3Hunna"**: Chief Keef, *3Hunna* (Santa Monica, CA: GBE Entertainment/Interscope, 2012).

152   **"In a strange linguistic trick"**: "On Being #3hunna and the Small Things That Define a Championship," *FSU News,* January 3, 2014, http: //www.fsunews.com/article/20140103/FSVIEW0201/140103011/On -being-3hunn-small-things-define-championship-team.

153   **retained an outside consultant**: Florida State University, statement provided to author.

154   **"online courses are under a lot of scrutiny"**: David Paradice, email message to Jane Ohlin, January 7, 2014.

154 **"the one thing I desperately need"**: Jane Ohlin, email message to Joanna Southerland, October 10, 2013.

154 **"her work ethic is above reproach"**: Jane Ohlin, email message to Susann Rudasill, December 13, 2013.

154 **Dr. Ohlin was overruled**: ibid.

154 **"Hello Sam"**: Christie Suggs, email message to Sam McCall, December 31, 2013.

156 **got out her garnet and gold**: Ashley Witherspoon, interview with author.

157 **"We need to be addressing this"**: ibid.

157 **"the atmosphere and environment"**: Matt Hauswirth, "Spotlight: Jimbo Fisher Wins National Championship for Florida State," *State Journal* (Charleston, WV), January 7, 2014.

158 **sang a line together**: Jameis Winston, Instagram post, posted February 2014, https://www.instagram.com/jaboowins5.

158 **"On the Floor"**: IceJJFish, "IceJJFish—On the Floor (Official Music Video)," posted February 6, 2014, https://www.youtube.com/watch?v=iq_d8VSM0nw.

CHAMPIONS

160 **posted a shot**: Instagram post, posted 2014, https://www.instagram.com/8ball_jones.

160 **"confirms you have provided impermissible benefits"**: Letter from University of North Carolina Athletics Director Richard A. Baddour to Anthony Machado, October 25, 2010.

160 **thirty thousand people**: Kareem Copeland, "Florida State Celebrates 3rd National Title," Associated Press, February 1, 2014.

161 **"This means you aren't just the greatest team"**: Arek Sarkissian II, "FSU Football Champs Receive Resolution From Tallahassee City Commission," *Tallahassee Democrat,* January 8, 2014.

161 **"He's very mature"**: Danny Aller, "FSU's Rashad Greene Making Albany, Westover Proud with Trip to Title Game," *Albany (GA) Herald,* January 4, 2014.

161 **"not enough enthusiasm"**: Corey Clark, "Fisher Not Thrilled With First Scrimmage," *Tallahassee Democrat,* April 1, 2014.

162 **"You can constantly hear them screaming"**: Mike McIntire and Walt Bogdanich, "At Florida State, Football Clouds Justice," *New York Times*, October 10, 2014. Also Tallahassee Police Department Incident Report No. 14-002727.

162   **boyfriend was Tre' Jackson**: Tallahassee Police Incident Report No. 14-002727.

163   **"due to the fact that it was an FSU football player"**: ibid.

163   **"Hart has become a very big man"**: Jason Staples, "Scouting the 2014 Seminoles: Bobby Hart," *Nole Digest*, July 7, 2014, http://www .scout.com/college/florida-state/story/1418916-scouting-the-2014- seminoles-bobby-hart.

163   **On the evening of February 9**: Tallahassee Police Incident Report No. 14-003926.

164   **"When I saw that, it was a red flag"**: Bud Elliott, "Ira Denson dismissed from Florida State football," *Tomahawk Nation*, March 19, 2014, http://www.tomahawknation.com/2014/1/10/5294872/florida -state-ira-denson-transfer-dismissed-guard-recruit.

165   **It was not until early March**: "Man Arrested for Attempted Homicide Involving FSU Football Players," WTXL-TV, March 7, 2014, http:// www.wtxl.com/news/local/man-arrested-for-attempted-homicide -involving-fsu-football-players/article_d6c26f5e-a61c-11e3-89ff -0017a43b2370.html.

165   **"We're going to evaluate how he does"**: Bob Ferrante, "Shooting Reportedly Tied to Dispute Between FSU Teammates," Fox Sports, March 7, 2014, http://www.foxsports.com/florida/story/dispute- between-fsu-teammates-reportedly-tied-to-shooting-030714.

165   **Denson himself was finally charged**: Nick Bromberg, "Florida State OL Ira Denson Arrested for Theft After Allegedly Using Teammate's Credit Card," Yahoo Sports, March 19, 2014, https://sports.yahoo .com/blogs/ncaaf-dr-saturday/florida-state-ol-ira-denson-arrested -for-theft-after-allegedly-using-teammate-s-credit-card-210529592 .html.

165   **thirteen years in prison**: Karl Etters, "Former FSU OL Ira Denson Sentenced to Probation," *Tallahassee Democrat*, September 18, 2015.

165   **five years' probation**: ibid.

165   **The officer pulled her gun**: Tallahassee Police Department Arrest/Probable Cause Affidavit for Delmarick Pender, Case No. 2016CF001366.

166   **"We're OK at running back"**: Brendan Sonnone, "FSU is 'OK' at Running Back Without Mario Pender, Jimbo Fisher Says," *Orlando Sentinel,* May 11, 2016.

166   **When he arrived at the seafood counter**: Leon County Sheriff's Office General Offense/Incident Report No. 140046813.

167   **"youthful ignorance"**: Michael David Smith, "Jameis Winston Blames 'Youthful Ignorance' for 'Terrible Mistake,'" NBC Sports,

April 30, 2014, http://profootballtalk.nbcsports.com/2014/04/30/jameis-winston-blames-youthful-ignorance-for-terrible-mistake/.

167 **A year later**: "Jameis Winston: Store Employee 'Hooked us up' With Crab Legs," ESPN, April 22, 2015, http://www.espn.com/nfl/draft 2015/story/_/id/12739843/jameis-winston-florida-state-seminoles -says-crab-legs-were-given-not-stolen.

167 **In broad daylight**: Mike McIntire and Walt Bogdanich, "At Florida State, Football Clouds Justice," *New York Times*, October 10, 2014.

167 **Frightened residents ducked**: Tallahassee Police Department Incident Report No. 14-017595.

168 **BB gun fights weren't**: McIntire and Bodganich, "At Florida State." Also Tallahassee Police Department Incident Report No. 14-016544.

170 **"Well I had my first"**: Samer Kalaf, "Jameis Winston Yells 'Fuck Her Right in the Pussy,' Killing Meme," *Deadspin*, September 16, 2014, http://deadspin.com/jameis-winston-yells-fuck-her-right-in-the -pussy-kil-1635466887.

170 **"As the university's most visible ambassadors"**: Jared Shanker, "FSU to Sit Jameis Winston for Half," ESPN, September 18, 2014, http:// www.espn.com/college-football/story/_/id/11542412/florida-state- seminoles-qb-jameis-winston-suspended-first-half-game-clemson- tigers-shouting-obscene-phrase-public.

171 **extended for a full game**: Jared Shanker, "Jameis Winston to Sit Whole Game," ESPN, September 20, 2014, http://www.espn.com/ college-football/story/_/id/11555354/jameis-winston-florida-state -seminoles-banned-entire-game-vs-clemson-tigers.

171 **College student Ian Keith**: Mike McIntire and Walt Bogdanich, "Florida State Player Fled Crash But Got Only Traffic Tickets," *New York Times*, November 14, 2014. Also State of Florida Department of Highway Safety & Motor Vehicles Traffic Crash Report No. 85039938.

173 **pictures of her bruised arm**: Brendan Sonnone, "FSU Tailback Karlos Williams Under Police Investigation for Alleged Domestic Battery," *Orlando Sentinel*, October 27, 2014.

173 **telling the police in an email**: Tallahassee Police Department Incident Report No. 14-030601.

173 **"We're not giving any credence"**: Jared Shanker, "Karlos Williams Investigation Over," ESPN, November 12, 2014, http://www.espn.com/ college-football/story/_/id/11865928/police-no-longer-investigating- karlos-williams-florida-state-seminoles-alleged-domestic-assault.

173 **A couple of weeks before Christmas**: Tallahassee Police Department Incident Report No. 14-035569.

176   **"They were all laughing"**: K.F., interview with author.

177   **"I am in fear"**: Petition for Injunction for Protection Against Dating Violence, Respondent Bobby Hart, Case No. 2014DR3593, Circuit Court, Second Judicial Circuit for Leon County, Florida.

NO. 24

181   **popped up on display**: "Seminoles Honor Seminoles," *Sun-Sentinel* (Fort Lauderdale, FL), May 7, 2014.

181   **emblems deemed offensive**: Robert Andrew Powell, "Florida State Can Keep Its Seminoles," *New York Times,* April 24, 2005.

182   **world's largest gambling enterprises**: "About the Seminole Tribe," Seminole Gaming, http://www.theseminolecasinos.com/about-us.

182   **online sports betting**: "The Dominican Republic's Best Sports Book," Hard Rock Hotel & Casino Punta Cana, http://www.hardrockhotel puntacana.com/sports-book.htm.

182   **"gambling & casinos"**: "Kyle Doney—LinkedIn," https://www.linked in.com/in/kyle-doney-85250b38.

182   **NCAA's strict guidelines**: "The NCAA's Advertising and Promotional Guidelines," NCAA, September 2016, http://i.turner.ncaa.com/ sites/default/files/images/2016/10/21/advertising_promotional_ standards_2016_revision_10-04-16.pdf.

183   **multibillion-dollar gambling enterprise**: Chabeli Herrera, "How the Seminole Tribe Came to Rock the Hard Rock Empire," *Miami Herald,* May 22, 2016.

183   **$5 billion a year**: ibid.

183   **its own aircraft**: "FAA Registry—Aircraft—N-Number Inquiry," Federal Aviation Administration, http://registry.faa.gov/aircraftinquiry/ NNum_Results.aspx?NNumbertxt=407ST.

183   **annual tribal festival**: Beverly Bidney, "FSU, Tribe celebrate football championship," *Seminole Tribune,* February 28, 2014, http://www .semtribe.com/seminoletribune/Archive/2014/SeminoleTribune_ February 28_2014v2.pdf.

183   **joining the exodus**: Steve Megargee, "Record Number of Underclassmen Declare," *Tallahassee Democrat,* January 16, 2014.

184   **posted a rant**: Devonta Freeman, Instagram post, posted January 2014, https://www.instagram.com/devontafreeman.

185   **"They are not business-savvy"**: Luther Campbell, "Sports Agents Take Advantage of African-American Football Players," *Miami New Times*, December 16, 2014.

185   **keynote speaker**: "Nova Southeastern Sports & Entertainment Law

Symposium," *Sports Agent Blog*, February 11, 2011, http://sportsagent
blog.com/2011/02/11/nova-southeastern-sports-entertainment-law
-symposium/.

185   **Sitting on the panel**: ibid.

185   **contract advice**: "Services," 40 Sports & Entertainment Group, http:
//40seg.com/services/.

185   **"Sports agents are thrown off their game"**: Campbell, "Sports Agents
Take Advantage."

186   **Among her clients**: "Clients," 40 Sports & Entertainment Group, http:
//40seg.com/clients/.

186   NCAA **rules forbid players**: NCAA, "12.3.1 Use of Agents," in *Division I Manual, 2016–17* (Indianapolis: National Collegiate Athletic
Association, 2016).

186   **"or anyone else who wishes"**: University of Missouri Department of
Intercollegiate Athletics, *Professional Sports Counseling Panel*, http://grfx
.cstv.com/photos/schools/miss/genrel/auto_pdf/counseling-panel.pdf.

187   **$2.7 million contract**: Vaughn McClure, "Rookie Devonta Freeman
Already Beat Odds," ESPN, July 30, 2014, http://www.espn.com/
blog/nflnation/post/_/id/133341/rookie-devonta-freeman-already
-beat-odds.

187   **"Me personally, I don't want nothing"**: ibid.

187   **"What an effort!"**: New Orleans Saints at Atlanta Falcons, *The NFL
on Fox*, Fox Broadcasting Company, September 7, 2014, http://ww.nfl
.com/gamecenter/2014090700/2014/REG1/saints@falcons/.

187   **"He's 6'5, play for"**: Luther Campbell, Instagram post, posted September 2014, https://www.instagram.com/unclelukereall1/

GETTING A BOOST

188   **white-haired sixty-four-year-old**: Sanford Lovingood, transcript of
videotaped interview with Leon County Sheriff's Office Detective
Jared Lee, recorded October 1, 2014, Case No. 14CF3001, Circuit
Court of the Second Judicial Circuit, Leon County, Florida.

188   **assets totaling $264 million**: Mike McIntire and Walt Bogdanich, "At
Florida State, Football Clouds Justice," *New York Times*, October 10,
2014.

189   **"I've never gotten"**: "FSU Board of Trustees Meeting, November 1,
2011," Florida State University Board of Trustees, November 1, 2011,
http://learningforlife.capd.fsu.edu/bot/nov1_11.htm.

189   **maneuver to steal**: State vs. Sanford Lovingood, case No. 14CF3001,
Circuit Court of the Second Judicial Circuit, Leon County, Florida.

189 **"You need to put some Jack Daniel's"**: Lovingood interview with Detective Lee.

190 **eight years in prison**: Karl Etters, "Former Boosters' Lovingood Sentenced to 8 Years in Prison," *Tallahassee Democrat*, October 9, 2015.

191 **former assistant coach**: Lanetra Bennett, "Authorities: Former FSU Booster Fell Out of Jail Transport Van," WCTV-TV, October 9, 2015, http://www.wctv.tv/home/headlines/Former-FSU-Booster -Sentenced-to-8-Years-331675641.html.

191 **"verified that all gifts"**: Karl Etters, "FSU Boosters: Former Comptroller Acted Alone in Theft," *Tallahassee Democrat*, January 31, 2015.

191 **"All of that is donor"**: Lovingood interview with Detective Lee.

191 **"promote the education"**: Seminole Boosters Inc., IRS Form 990, Return of Organization Exempt from Income Tax.

191 **"I don't know what we'd do"**: "FSU Board of Trustees Meeting, September 9, 2011," Florida State Board of Trustees, http://learningfor life.capd.fsu.edu/bot/sept9_11.htm.

191 **buy out the contract**: Emily Badger, "Jeff Bowden Receives Nice Parting Gift," *Orlando Sentinel*, November 16, 2006.

191 **Boosters also paid about $70,000**: Brent Kallestad, "FSU Spends More Than $172,000 on lawyers," Associated Press, May 25, 2010.

192 **private donations for athletics**: Data from the Council for Aid to Education's Voluntary Support for Education Survey, researched by the author.

192 **helped pay the chancellor's salary**: Records of the Jamail Regents' Chair in Higher Education Leadership, University of Texas System.

193 **"and that's a lot of money"**: John Spong, "A Season in Hell," *Texas Monthly*, January 2014.

193 **"Tell them to send me"**: ibid.

193 **Ereck Plancher collapsed**: "Out of the Sunshine, Shielded in Shadow—The Oracle," First Amendment Foundation, http://florida faf.org/sunshine-shielded-shadow-oracle/.

194 **first year of operation**: Crimson Tide Foundation, IRS Form 990, Return of Organization Exempt from Income Tax, 2004.

194 **sixty-five-page financial report**: University of Alabama, *Financial Report, 2012–13*, https://finance-estus.fa.ua.edu/FinancialAccounting/ FAPPub/UA Financial Reports/ua-finanical-report-12-13.pdf.

194 **spent $3 million**: Kent Faulk, "Nick Saban Sold Home to Crimson Tide Foundation for $3.1 Million in 2013," *Birmingham News*, October 26, 2014.

194 **highest-paid public employee**: Leada Gore, "Nick Saban is the High-

est Paid Public Employee in America," *Birmingham News,* September 21, 2016.

195 **search for a successor**: "Your Presidential Search Advisory Committee," FSU Progress Coalition, September 22, 2014, https://fsu progresscoalition.wordpress.com/page/2/.

195 **funnel millions each year**: Florida State University Department of Athletics, *Financial Statements June 30, 2013,* & 2012.

195 **Southern Strategy Group**: "Team," Southern Strategy Group, http:// sostrategy.com/team/.

195 **Kidz1stFund**: "Our Mission," Kidz1stFund, http://www.kidz1stfund .com/our-mission/.

196 **firing a shotgun**: Mike McIntire and Walt Bogdanich, "At Florida State, Football Clouds Justice," *New York Times,* October 10, 2014.

196 **"exclusive experience"**: Old School Open brochure, http://old schoolopen.com/form_pdf/OldSchoolOpenBrochureV2.pdf.

196 **nine members of the Boosters**: Dave Hodges, "College Town Has Great Potential—and Risks," Capital Trust Agency Community Development Entity LLC, http://ctacde.com/news/post?s=1969-12 -31-college-town-project-has-great-potential-and-risks.

197 **demanded to see her file**: Deposition of Melissa Ashton, Erica Kinsman v. Florida State University Board of Trustees, Case No. 6:15-cv-00235, U.S. District Court for the Middle District of Florida, June 24, 2015.

197 **"Turning them over made me extremely uncomfortable"**: ibid.

198 **"Both, Your Honor"**: Transcript of Investigative Hearing Before Justice Major Harding, Florida State University, December 3, 2014.

198 **"In light of all the circumstances"**: Iliana Limon Romero and Brendan Sonnone, "No Code of Conduct Violation for Winston," *Orlando Sentinel,* December 22, 2014.

199 **"It's all about a football game"**: Associated Press, "Accuser's Lawyer: 'Fix Was In' with Winston Code of Conduct Hearing," December 23, 2014.

199 **slated to keep $700,000**: Rachel Axon, "Did FSU Overstate Attorney's Fees in Announcing Lawsuit Settlement?" *USA Today,* January 25, 2016.

199 **kept on his desk**: Tom D'Angelo, "FSU President John Thrasher on Offensive to Defend School's Image," *Palm Beach (FL) Post,* February 7, 2015.

200 **settlement was being paid**: Sean Rossman and Byron Dobson, "FSU Reaches Settlement with Winston's Accuser," *Tallahassee Democrat,* January 26, 2016.

CHRISTIE

201   **"I can't stress enough"**: Melissa Isaak, interview with author.

202   **Christie's life only became**: Petition for Support and Other Relief,
      State vs. Philbert C. Suggs, "Petition for Support and Other Relief."
      Case No.14001092DR.

203   **She wouldn't wake up**: Melissa Isaak and Phil Suggs, interviews with
      author.

203   **rule her death an accident**: Autopsy Report for Christina Suggs, Dis-
      trict Fourteen Medical Examiner, Case No. 2014-MLA-0393.

203   **"Do you think"**: Melissa Isaak, interview with author.

AFTERWORD

207   **"doesn't want to deal"**: Gerald Gurney, interview with author.

207   **"Clearly, there are academic integrity issues here"**: ibid.

209   **"The NFL and NBA"**: confidential source, interview by author.

INDEX